Decodable Takehome Books

Level 3

A Division of The McGraw·Hill Companies

Columbus, Ohio

www.sra4kids.com

SRA/McGraw-Hill 

A Division of The ***McGraw·Hill*** *Companies*

Printed in the United States of America.

Send all inquiries to:
SRA/McGraw-Hill
8787 Orion Place
Columbus, OH 43240-4027

ISBN 0-07-572389-1
2 3 4 5 6 7 8 9 QPD 06 05 04 03 02

Contents

Level 3

About the Decodable Takehome Books 5–6
Parent Letter 7

1 Dave the Brave 9–12
2 Sleepy Steve 13–16
3 The Shy Bird's Trick 17–20
4 Chinlow of Singboat 21–24
5 Mrs. Music 25–28
6 Paul, Aunt Maud, and Claude 29–32
7 Flower the Cow 33–36
8 Toy Store Explorer 37–40
9 A Book for Mr. Hook 41–44
10 Root Stew 45–48
11 The Frog Who Wanted to Fly 49–56
12 Up to Bat 57–64
13 Baking Princess 65–72
14 City Girl 73–80
15 The Prince's Foolish Wish 81–88
16 Rose the Brave 89–96
17 Hugo Bugle 97–104
18 Queen Kit 105–112
19 Dead as a Dodo, Bald as an Eagle 113–120
20 The Lives of Sea Turtles 121–128
21 Nesting and Burrowing Birds 129–136
22 Loop and Hook a Dream 137–144
23 Sweet and Sour Soup 145–152
24 No Noise! 153–160
25 Summer Pen Pals 161–168
26 Joyce Writes a Good Story 169–176
27 Little Hare 177–184
28 Ralph, a Bug 185–192
29 Kitty and the Nothing Day 193–200
30 Traveling Star 201–208
31 Whales 209–216
32 The Stone Wall 217–224
33 Say It in Code 225–232
34 Peace and Quiet 233–240
35 School Days Long Ago 241–248

About the Decodable Takehome Books

The *SRA Open Court Reading Decodable Books* allow your students to apply their knowledge of phonic elements to read simple, engaging texts. Each story supports instruction in a new phonic element and incorporates elements and words that have been learned earlier.

The students can fold and staple the pages of each *Decodable Takehome Book* to make books of their own to keep and read. We suggest that you keep extra sets of the stories in your classroom for the children to reread.

How to make a Decodable Takehome Book

1. Tear out the pages you need.

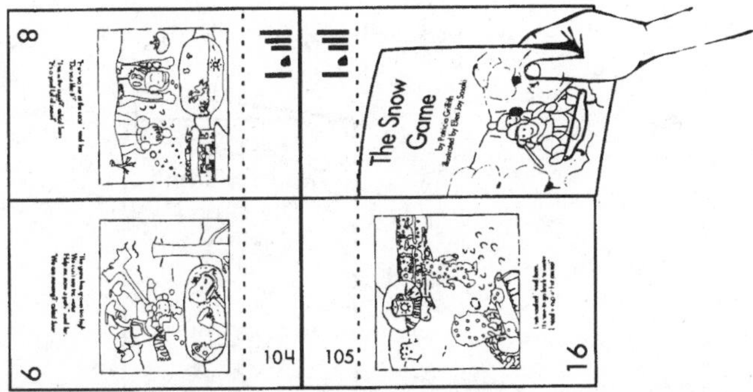

2. For 16-page stories, place pages 8 and 9, 6 and 11, 4 and 13, and 2 and 15 faceup.

or

2. For 8-page stories, place pages 4 and 5, and pages 2 and 7 faceup.

For 16-page book

3. Place the pages on top of each other in this order: pages 8 and 9, pages 6 and 11, pages 4 and 13, and pages 2 and 15.

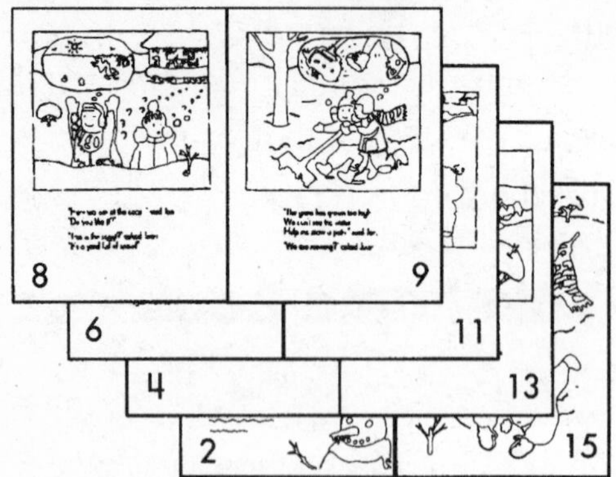

4. Fold along the center line.

5. Check to make sure the pages are in order.

6. Staple the pages along the fold.

For 8-page book

3. Place pages 4 and 5 on top of pages 2 and 7.

4. Fold along the center line.

5. Check to make sure the pages are in order.

6. Staple the pages along the fold.

Just to let you know...

A message from ______________________________

Help your child discover the joy of independent reading with *SRA Open Court Reading*. From time to time your child will bring home his or her very own *Decodable Takehome Books* to share with you. With your help, these stories can give your child important reading practice and a joyful shared reading experience.

You may want to set aside a few minutes every evening to read these stories together. Here are some suggestions you may find helpful:

- Do not expect your child to read each story perfectly, but concentrate on sharing the book together.
- Participate by doing some of the reading.
- Talk about the stories as you read, give lots of encouragement, and watch as your child becomes more fluent throughout the year!

Learning to read takes lots of practice. Sharing these stories is one way that your child can gain that valuable practice. Encourage your child to keep the *Decodable Takehome Books* in a special place. This collection will make a library of books that your child can read and reread. Take the time to listen to your child read from his or her library. Just a few moments of shared reading each day can give your child the confidence needed to excel in reading.

Children who read every day come to think of reading as a pleasant, natural part of life. One way to inspire your child to read is to show that reading is an important part of your life by letting him or her see you reading books, magazines, newspapers, or any other materials. Another good way to show that you value reading is to share a *Decodable Takehome Book* with your child each day.

Successful reading experiences allow children to be proud of their new-found reading ability. Support your child with interest and enthusiasm about reading. You won't regret it!

"You're brave, Val," said Dave.
"Yes, Dave," said Val, "but will I ever be as brave as you?"

Dave the Brave

by Ana Rojas
illustrated by Len Epstein

Book 1

A Division of The McGraw-Hill Companies
Columbus, Ohio

SRA OPEN COURT READING

www.sra4kids.com

SRA/McGraw-Hill

A Division of The ***McGraw-Hill*** *Companies*

Printed in the United States of America.

Send all inquiries to:
SRA/McGraw-Hill
8787 Orion Place
Columbus, OH 43240-4027

Just then a big snake came up to Dave and Val.

"I'm afraid of snakes!" said Dave.

"Scram, snake, scram!" yelled Val. She chased the snake.

"I raced a truck on a dirt trail," said Dave.
"But, Dave," said Val, "you can't race."

"I am the bravest!" Dave said. "Today, I swam across a lake to save a dog."

"But, Dave," said his little sister, Val, "you can't swim."

"I came face-to-face with a big cat in Africa," said Dave.

"But, Dave," said Val, "you are scared of cats."

"I saved a snake from a dragon," said Dave.

"But, Dave," said Val, "you hate snakes."

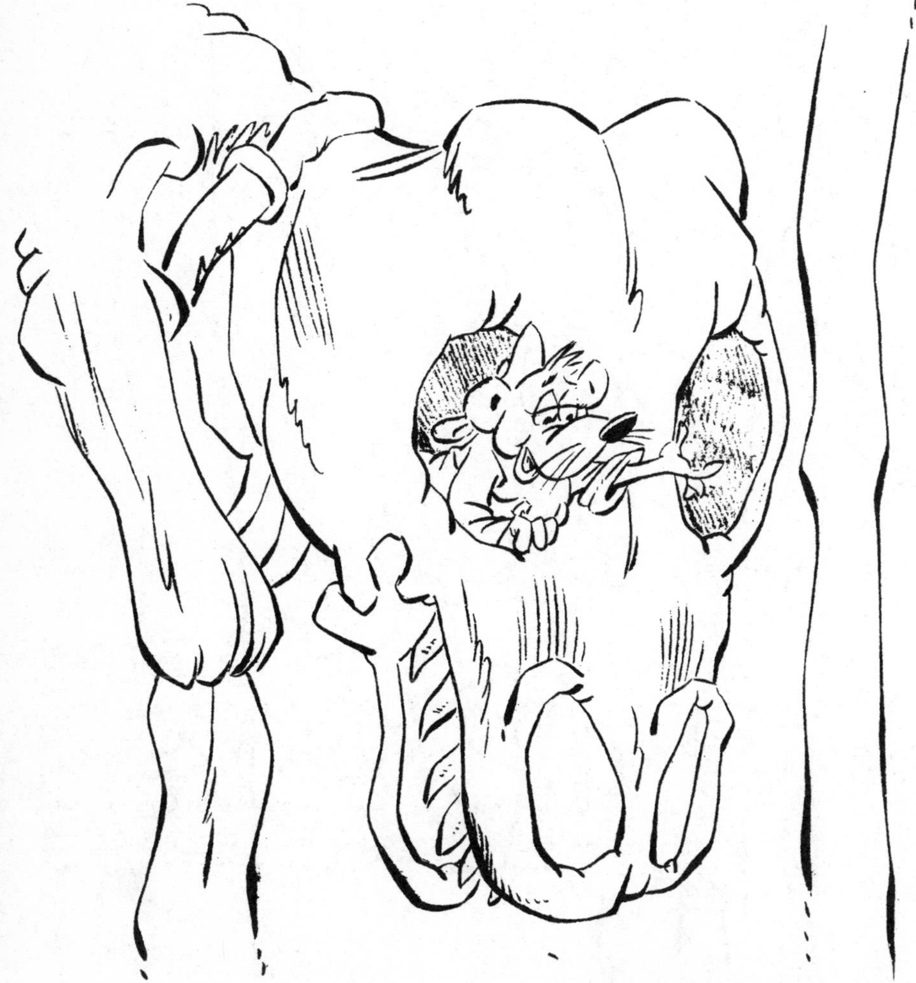

Steve climbed up the dinosaur and made a neat nest. "Pleased to meet you," whispered Steve. And the two new pals settled into a deep peaceful sleep.

Sleepy Steve

by Peter Matheny
illustrated by Len Epstein

Book 2

A Division of The McGraw-Hill Companies

Columbus, Ohio

SRA OPEN COURT READING

www.sra4kids.com

SRA/McGraw-Hill

A Division of The McGraw-Hill Companies

Printed in the United States of America.

Send all inquiries to:
SRA/McGraw-Hill
8787 Orion Place
Columbus, OH 43240-4027

Then Steve saw a sign near the sticks. "Dinosaurs?" said Steve. "These sticks are a large dinosaur!"

When Steve was awake, he came from beneath the sticks. He peeked back at them.

"Please tell me what you are," Steve said to the sticks.

But the sticks did not speak.

Sleepy Steve was afraid. He hurried into a big building and hid beneath a heap of sticks.

"I am free!" Steve eeked. "But I am very sleepy! I need a place to sleep!"

Sleepy Steve peeked out from beneath the sticks. "Eeek!" said Steve. He saw big sticks. He saw little sticks. Steve was afraid.

Sleepy Steve began to sneak past the sticks. "Eeek!" said Steve. He saw big feet. He saw little feet.

He leaned back and fell asleep where he was.

"See, Fox," sighed the shy bird, "you are sly, but not as sly as I."

"Bye-bye, sly Fox!" cried the bird, and she flew off into the sky.

The Shy Bird's Trick

by Wiley
illustrated by Kersti Frigell

Book 3

A Division of The McGraw-Hill Companies

Columbus, Ohio

SRA OPEN COURT READING

www.sra4kids.com

SRA/McGraw-Hill

A Division of The **McGraw-Hill** *Companies*

Printed in the United States of America.

Send all inquiries to:
SRA/McGraw-Hill
8787 Orion Place
Columbus, OH 43240-4027

"I will help you," replied the shy bird. "Hold the string with your long tail while I tie it," she said to the fox.

Then, the shy bird tied the fox's tail to the box in a tight knot.

"My tail is stuck!" grumbled the fox.

"Is that a lie?" asked the shy bird.

"Oh, no," cried the sly fox as he licked his lips. "I need your help."

"I'll bet there is no pie in that box," the shy bird mumbled. "I'll bet that sly fox wants *me* to be the pie!"

Once a sly fox lived deep in the forest. The sly fox was very hungry.

"I might die of hunger!" he cried.

Then, the sly fox spied a bird flying in the sky.

"I will trick this bird," said the sly fox. "It will make a nice pie."

"Oh, shy little bird," called the sly fox. "You look tired. Come and lie on my soft fur."

The bird in the sky didn't say anything.

"Sweet, shy bird," said the sly fox. "I need your help to tie this string on my pie box. Inside is a yummy pie for my mother."

Finally, the emperor called Chinlow to him. "Show me," he said. Chinlow looked into the face of a tiny rose. The rose grew and became lovely. Then the emperor said to Chinlow, "Now look at me."

Chinlow looked into the emperor's eyes. The emperor saw love in her eyes. "Now I know her talent," he said, "and I am not afraid of it. Her talent is love."

Chinlow of Singboat

by Jo Olson
illustrated by Pat Lucas-Morris

Book 4

A Division of The McGraw-Hill Companies
Columbus, Ohio

www.sra4kids.com

SRA/McGraw-Hill

A Division of The **McGraw·Hill** *Companies*

Printed in the United States of America.

Send all inquiries to:
SRA/McGraw-Hill
8787 Orion Place
Columbus, OH 43240-4027

Chinlow looked into the face of a tiny rose. The rose Chinlow looked at began to grow until it became the loveliest rose in the garden.

Each teacher said, "I saw her talent, but I do not know it."

The emperor called for his wisest teachers. "I must know," he said, "the talent of Chinlow."

One by one the teachers spoke to Chinlow. "Show me," each teacher said.

In the little village of Singboat lived a girl named Chinlow. She loved nature. Nature loved her.

The birds of the forest sang more sweetly for her. The doe of the forest ate from her hand. The snow on the hills shone whitest for her.

The roses Chinlow planted would always grow tall.

"Where does Chinlow's talent come from?" people of the village asked. "Even the rainbow is more dazzling over Chinlow's home."

News of Chinlow's talent reached the emperor in faraway Pancoat.

"Could the talent of a simple child overthrow the emperor?" he wondered. "I must not let this go on."

The next day Mrs. Music and Stu went for their walk.

"Oh, my!" said Mrs. Music when she saw the bugle. "Stu, look at that beautiful bugle! I wonder where I can put it?"

Mrs. Music

by Carolyn Crimi
illustrated by Anthony Accardo

Book 5

A Division of The McGraw-Hill Companies
Columbus, Ohio

SRA OPEN COURT READING

www.sra4kids.com

SRA/McGraw-Hill
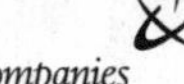
A Division of The ***McGraw-Hill*** *Companies*

Printed in the United States of America.

Send all inquiries to:
SRA/McGraw-Hill
8787 Orion Place
Columbus, OH 43240-4027

Later that day Mr. Quinlan came by with his cart. "What a beautiful clock!" he cried. "It must be valuable. I will take it home."

But Mr. Quinlan's cart was full. "A cleaning is needed," Mr. Quinlan said. "I don't use this bugle anymore. I will throw it away."

Hugo put the candlesticks on Aunt Iris's shelf. The candlesticks were beautiful, but the shelf was full.

"Hugo," said Aunt Iris, "a cleaning is needed! I don't use this clock anymore. I have quite a few others. I will throw this one away."

Every day Mrs. Music and her cat Stu went for a stroll.

"Look!" Mrs. Music said one day to Stu. "Someone has thrown a beautiful dish into the trash! That dish would look grand on my table."

Mrs. Music rushed home and put the dish on her table. The dish was beautiful, but the table was full.

"Stu," said Mrs. Music, "a cleaning is needed! I don't use these candlesticks anymore. I will throw them away."

Hugo was walking home from work when he saw the candlesticks.

"What unusual candlesticks!" he said to himself. "They must have come from a museum. Aunt Iris would love them!"

Hugo picked up the candlesticks and took them to his aunt.

"You found him!" said Aunt Maud happily. "You returned my pet tiger!"

Aunt Maud gave the exhausted Claude a kiss. Then she turned to Paul. "Now can you help me find my pet lion?"

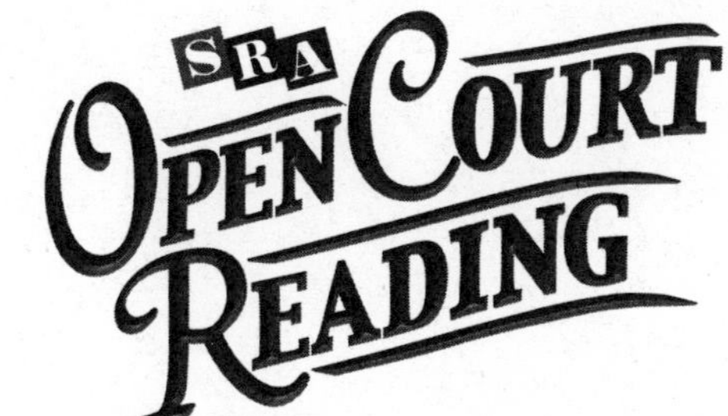

Paul, Aunt Maud, and Claude

by Carolyn Crimi
illustrated by Kersti Frigell

Book 6

A Division of The McGraw-Hill Companies

Columbus, Ohio

www.sra4kids.com

SRA/McGraw-Hill

A Division of The **McGraw-Hill** *Companies*

Printed in the United States of America.

Send all inquiries to:
SRA/McGraw-Hill
8787 Orion Place
Columbus, OH 43240-4027

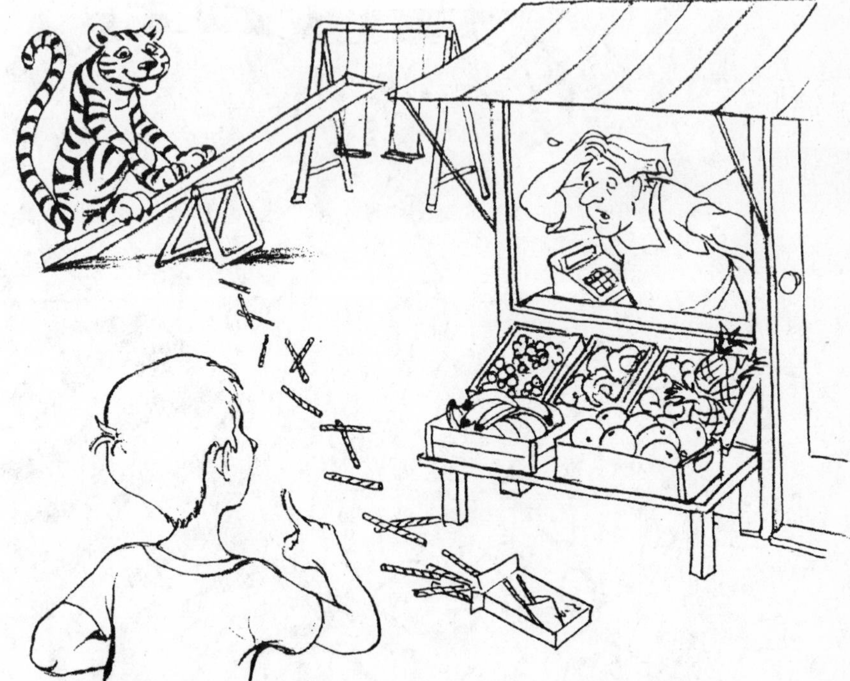

Outside the store, Paul saw an open box of straws.

"Claude must have been here, too!" said Paul. He followed the straws until he came to the playground. There sat Claude on the seesaw.

"You must be hungry, Claude," said Paul cautiously.

Paul gave Claude some sausage. Then, with a trail of raw cauliflower, he slowly led the tiger back home.

One day Aunt Maud looked distraught.
"Claude must be lost!" she said.
"I can help," said Paul.
Paul ran across Maud's lawn to a dairy farm.
"These cows look awfully scared," thought Paul.
"I'll bet Claude has been here."
He looked down and saw buttermilk paw prints. He followed them to a nearby store.

Paul's aunt Maud owned a tiger named Claude.
Claude had four big paws with sharp claws.
"Claude is really quite tame," said Aunt Maud.
"I have even taught him tricks."

Paul watched as Claude performed his tricks. Claude could turn somersaults. He could balance on a seesaw. He could even do laundry!

"He must be an awfully smart tiger," thought Paul.

"How do you get Claude to do these tricks?" asked Paul.

"I feed him well," said Aunt Maud. "He likes to gnaw on sausages and raw cauliflower, and he loves to sip buttermilk through a straw."

33

Scooter looked around at the animals. They looked down at the ground.

"It sounds," said the mouse, "like some animals around here *are* too proud…but I doubt that Flower is one of them!"

SRA OPEN COURT READING

SRA OPEN COURT READING

Flower the Cow

by Dottie Raymer
illustrated by Deborah Colvin Borgo

Book 7

A Division of The McGraw-Hill Companies
Columbus, Ohio

www.sra4kids.com

SRA/McGraw-Hill

A Division of The **McGraw-Hill** *Companies*

Printed in the United States of America.

Send all inquiries to:
SRA/McGraw-Hill
8787 Orion Place
Columbus, OH 43240-4027

Finally, little Scooter the mouse spoke up. "Well, I don't know about plowing or rooting or laying eggs," she said. "But I do know that you can always count on Flower for just the right amount of sweet milk."

"Root around?" clucked the hens and other barnyard fowl. "That's nothing to be proud of. However, if she could lay eggs like ours, now *that* would be something to be proud of!"

Once a brown cow named Flower lived on a farm just outside of town.

Flower stayed mostly out in the field. She kept her head down and never seemed to notice the other animals around the farm.

"How can that cow be so proud?" Howdy the horse wondered aloud. "Why, she can't even pull a plow!"

"Pull a plow?" shouted Stout the sow. "That's nothing to be proud of! However, if she could root around in the ground with her snout, now *that* would be something to be proud of!"

Well, here is my choice. It's a bright plastic coil that does all kinds of tricks.

Toy Store Explorer

by Zena Smith
illustrated by Deborah Colvin Borgo

Book 8

A Division of The McGraw-Hill Companies

Columbus, Ohio

SRA Open Court Reading

www.sra4kids.com

SRA/McGraw-Hill

A Division of The **McGraw·Hill** *Companies*

Printed in the United States of America.

Send all inquiries to:
SRA/McGraw-Hill
8787 Orion Place
Columbus, OH 43240-4027

38

There's still so much more to see. There are games, books, jigsaw puzzles, and so many more toys. What can I choose?

There are shelves of dolls. They come in all shapes and sizes. Here's a princess in a royal gown. Another doll has a voice that sounds almost human.

I like to explore Roy's wonderful toy store.

Here's a shiny kite made completely of red, green, yellow, and blue foil. What a spectacular sight that would be in the sky!

Now here's another fine choice. It's a model of a ship. It's a destroyer. Look at all the pieces. I'd need glue to join them all.

Next is an oil truck with a cab and trailer. They come apart. It also has a flexible hose.

Lucy read her book to Mr. Hook every day. One day, the children came to play at the brook. "Why doesn't Mr. Hook yell at us anymore?" they asked Lucy's mother.

"He's got a new friend," she said.

"Who?" the children asked.

"Peter Pan," said Lucy's mother.

A Book for Mr. Hook

by Carolyn Crimi
illustrated by Kersti Frigell

Book 9

A Division of The McGraw-Hill Companies

Columbus, Ohio

SRA OPEN COURT READING

www.sra4kids.com

SRA/McGraw-Hill

A Division of The McGraw-Hill Companies

Printed in the United States of America.

Send all inquiries to:
SRA/McGraw-Hill
8787 Orion Place
Columbus, OH 43240-4027

Lucy and her mother took the book to Mr. Hook's house. "My teacher said I need to practice reading. May I read my book to you?"

"What book?" yelled Mr. Hook.

"*Peter Pan*," said Lucy.

"Hmm," said Mr. Hook. "Well, okay . . . "

Lucy took off the cloth. She went to her bookshelf and chose a book. "This is a good book," she said. "I'll bet Mr. Hook would like it."

Lucy's mother understood. "Good idea!" she said.

Once an old man named Mr. Hook lived by a brook in the woods. Whenever the children played by the brook, the old man yelled, "Stay away from my brook!"

"Why does he act like that?" Lucy asked her mother.

Lucy's mother said that Mr. Hook cannot see. She took a cloth and tied it across Lucy's eyes. "Here," she said. "Maybe this will help you understand how Mr. Hook feels."

Lucy tried putting on her shoes. She could not even find her foot.

Worst of all, Lucy could not read. "I don't know what I would do if I could not read books!" said Lucy.

Hunter flew closer and closer. "He's really in a bad mood tonight," said Bruce. "He must *hate* root stew!"

Scooter listened hard. Then he squeaked with glee! "Why, Hunter isn't calling 'Hoot, hoot, hoot!'" he exclaimed. "Hunter is calling 'Stew, stew, stew!'"

Root Stew

by Marie Foster
illustrated by Deborah Colvin Borgo

Book 10

A Division of The McGraw-Hill Companies

Columbus, Ohio

SRA OPEN COURT READING

www.sra4kids.com

SRA/McGraw-Hill

A Division of The McGraw-Hill Companies

Printed in the United States of America.

Send all inquiries to:
SRA/McGraw-Hill
8787 Orion Place
Columbus, OH 43240-4027

As the moon rose, Scooter and Bruce listened. In the distance, they heard Hunter's call. "Hoot, hoot, hoot! Hoot, hoot, hoot!"

"Rats!" said Scooter gloomily. "He didn't like the root stew."

The next day, Scooter worked. Into a pot he tossed chopped roots, berries, and shoots. That night, before the moon rose, Scooter crept over to Hunter's roost. There, he left the pot of root stew.

Scooter and Bruce lived in an old boot next to a blue pool. Most of the time, Scooter's and Bruce's lives went smoothly. During the day, they snoozed inside the cool boot. At night, they snooped for food.

The only time Scooter's and Bruce's lives did not go smoothly was when the moon was bright. When the moon was bright, they hid in the boot and listened for Hunter's "Hoot, hoot, hoot."

They knew that "Hoot, hoot, hoot" meant that Hunter was hungry. Mice were not safe when Hunter was hungry.

Scooter thought it was his duty to do something about Hunter.

"Hunter always seems hungry," he said, "and he always seems to be in a bad mood. Maybe Hunter isn't getting anything nice to eat."

"Well, I sat there and I thought—perhaps I can't fly, but maybe I can dive."

The Frog Who Wanted to Fly

by Barbara Seiger
illustrated by Kersti Frigell

Ivan Can't.................................3
Ivan Can.................................11

Book 11

A Division of The McGraw-Hill Companies

Columbus, Ohio

SRA OPEN COURT READING

www.sra4kids.com

SRA/McGraw-Hill

A Division of The McGraw-Hill Companies

Printed in the United States of America.

Send all inquiries to:
SRA/McGraw-Hill
8787 Orion Place
Columbus, OH 43240-4027

Ivan went home. He thought and thought. Then he brightened. He smiled. He danced a jig. He sang a silly song. Then he called his friend at the lab.

"I've made up my mind. This is what I want," he said.

Jane Triangle kept quiet while Ivan explained.

"But what if it's not right for me? I mean, I *am* a frog," said Ivan.

"A frog who fights for what he wants!" added Jane Triangle.

Jane Triangle smiled at Ivan, but Ivan did not smile back. "I can do frog things. Where's the fun in that?" he asked.

"I understand," said Jane Triangle.

"I want to do something I can't do," he said.

Ivan Can't

Once there was a tiny frog named Ivan. Ivan was not a happy frog. He sighed all the time.

"Why are you sighing?" asked Mr. Pie.

"All my life I've wanted to fly," said Ivan with a sigh.

"Why?" asked Mr. Pie.

"Why not?" said Ivan.

"Frogs can't fly," said Mr. Pie.

"This frog will," Ivan said.

Ivan decided to ask that nice Jane Triangle for help. She was a scientist. She'd tell him how to fly.

"You can jump," said Pam My-Oh-My. "You are the best jumper I've seen."

"You can swim," said Sy Bly. "You are the best swimmer I've seen."

"And you can grab trapped things with your long tongue," said Dan DeeLight.

"I can't think of anyone who can do all *that,*" said Jane Triangle.

"Why do you want to fly?" asked Jane Triangle.

"Who knows?" Ivan said. "But I think about it all the time. It's something I want. A lot," he added.

"Everyone needs something they want a lot," said Jane Triangle. "I wanted to be a scientist all my life. But . . . Ivan, might you be setting your sights too high? You are a *frog,* and frogs can't fly. Frogs do frog things."

"Like?" asked Ivan.

While on his way, Ivan heard his name.

"Hello-o-o-o-o! Ivan!" called Pam My-Oh-My. "Can you help me shut this trunk? The top will not shut tightly."

Ivan looked at the trunk. Then he got on top of it and jumped on it with all his might. The trunk shut tightly. "It's fine," he said.

Pam My-Oh-My smiled. "You are very nice. Can I get you mint ice cream?"

"No, thanks," said Ivan, "I'm off to see Jane Triangle. She will tell me how to fly."

"But frogs can't . . ."

"This frog will."

Ivan Can

While on his way, Ivan ran right into Jane Triangle herself!

"I was just on my way to see you," said Ivan.

"Well, here I am," said Jane Triangle.

"I want to fly," said Ivan. "You are a scientist. Can you help me?"

In no time, Ivan had slipped his long tongue under the top and picked up the stamp. "Here it is," smiled Ivan, the tenth stamp stuck to his tongue.

"Delightful, delightful," exclaimed Dan DeeLight.

While on his way, Ivan met Sy Bly. "I need to cross the pond," said Sy Bly. "Can you get me to that side?"

"Hop on my back," offered Ivan.

Sy Bly hopped on.

"Now hang on tightly," said Ivan, and he jumped into the pond.

"Are you all right?" Ivan asked when they had landed.

"I'm wet," Sy said. "But I'm fine. Thanks for the ride!"

While on his way, Ivan met Dan DeeLight. "Oh, no!" cried Dan DeeLight. "I'm sending cards to ten friends, inviting them to my party. But the tenth stamp is inside this desk. And—just my luck!—the top is stuck. I can't get the stamp!"

I was not sad.
I was not mad.
I was up to bat!

Up to Bat

by Robyn Pickering
illustrated by Gary Undercuffler

Gone 3
Map 11

Book 12

A Division of The McGraw-Hill Companies

Columbus, Ohio

SRA Open Court Reading

www.sra4kids.com

SRA/McGraw-Hill

A Division of The McGraw-Hill Companies

Printed in the United States of America.

Send all inquiries to:
SRA/McGraw-Hill
8787 Orion Place
Columbus, OH 43240-4027

And there were Len and Nan and Sal and Mat! Pam was there, too. I was out of breath. "Still mad?" she asked.

… there was my bat! There was my cap! There were my shoes! And Ben and Tam!

Gone

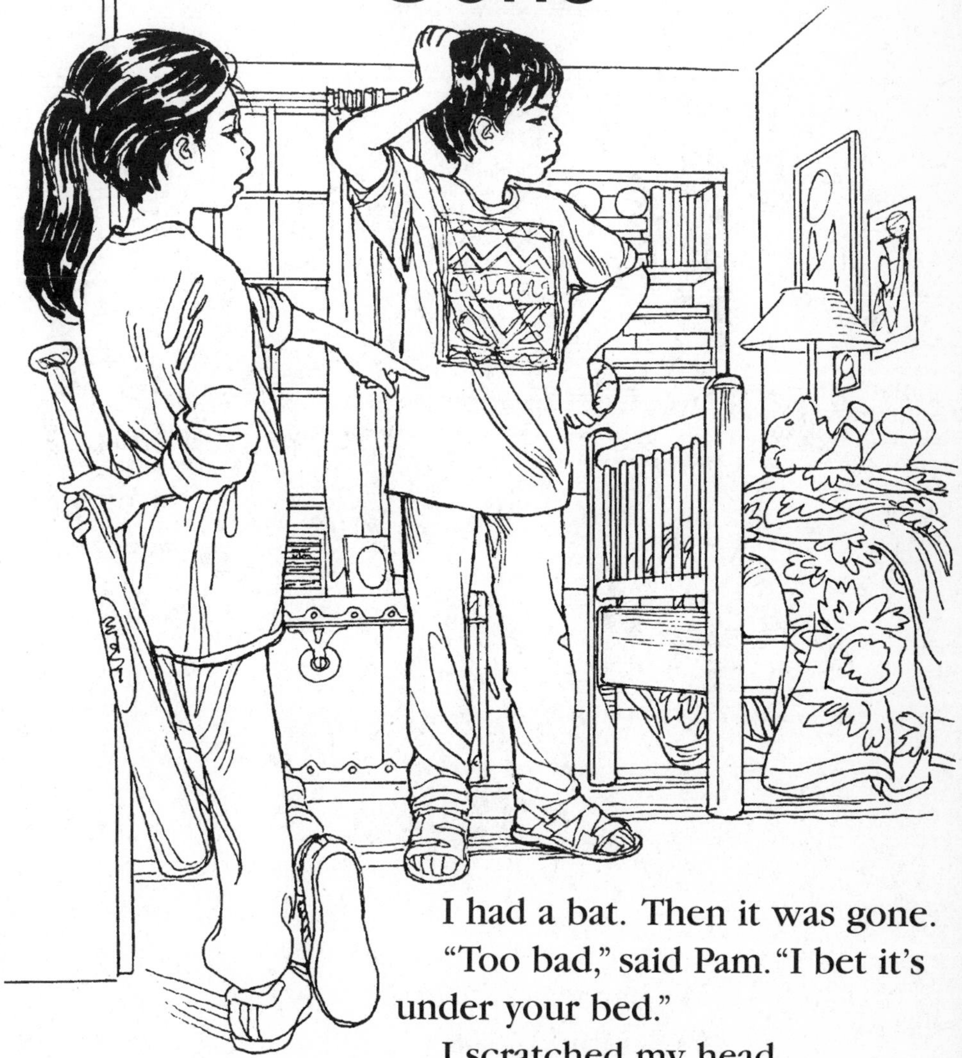

I had a bat. Then it was gone.

"Too bad," said Pam. "I bet it's under your bed."

I scratched my head.

My bat was not under my bed.
I grumbled.

So I ran fast past Dad. I ran fast past the ten hens in a pen. I ran fast past the man with the hat on his head—and …

On the map were Dad, ten hens in a pen, and a man with a hat on his head.

"What is this?" I mumbled. I was still mad.

"It's a map," said Pam. "It can help you get your bat, cap, and shoes back. And Ben and Tam."

I had a cap. Then it was gone. I held my breath.

"Too bad," said Pam. "I bet it's in the den."

My cap was not in the den. There were books I have read and a game of chess.

Map

"I can help get your bat, cap, and shoes back. And Ben and Tam," said Pam.

She gave me a map, which I read.

That did it! I was sad. I was mad. I was sad and mad. I was so mad I trembled.

"Tell me where my stuff is!" I said to Pam.

Pam ran.

"I had tan shoes. Then they were gone," I said with dread.

"Too bad," said Pam. "Ask Dad."

Dad did not have my tan shoes.
I was numb.

I had two best pals, Ben and Tam. They were gone, too.

"Too bad," said Pam. "I bet they went to run and climb and play."

The next day, Jake and Princess Fay made cakes and tarts.

At the end of the day, Fay gazed at Jake and said to herself, "Perhaps one day. . . ."

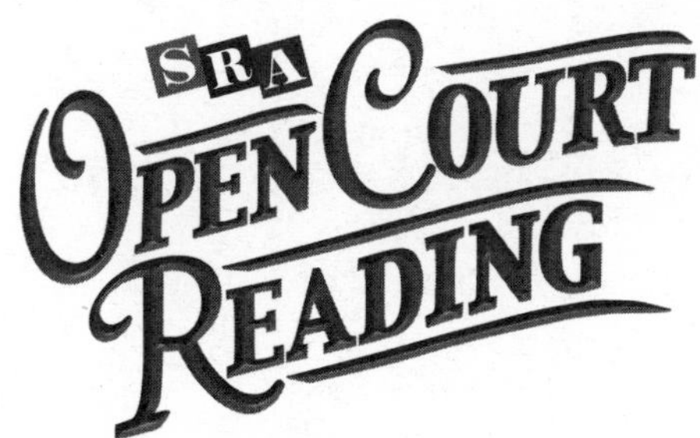

Baking Princess

by Barbara Seiger
illustrated by Kersti Frigell

Princess Fay Must Wed 3
The Contest 9

Book 13

A Division of The McGraw-Hill Companies
Columbus, Ohio

SRA OPEN COURT READING

www.sra4kids.com

SRA/McGraw-Hill

A Division of The McGraw-Hill Companies

Printed in the United States of America.

Send all inquiries to:
SRA/McGraw-Hill
8787 Orion Place
Columbus, OH 43240-4027

Jake and Princess Fay felt sad.

The king felt bad.

Then Fay felt glad.

"Dad," she said, "Let's rethink. I did not wish to wed yet. Let's make Jake the palace baker."

"Yes!" exclaimed King Raymund. "That is the perfect way to fix this problem!"

Then he turned to Jake, "You will bake with Princess Fay."

Princess Fay tasted the muffin. "Yum, yum," she said. And then, "Yes, yes, yes! This is the best cake I ever ate."

"But he is not a prince," added King Raymund.

"I don't care," said Princess Fay. "The princes did not bake cakes such as this."

SRA Open Court Reading

Princess Fay Must Wed

On Sunday, King Raymund went to Princess Fay and said, "It is time. You must wed. You spend too much time in this kitchen."

"I have no wish to wed," stated the princess. "But if I must, I wish to wed a baker! Then I can make cakes and tarts with him!"

"Remember, it must be a baker who is a prince," replied King Raymund.

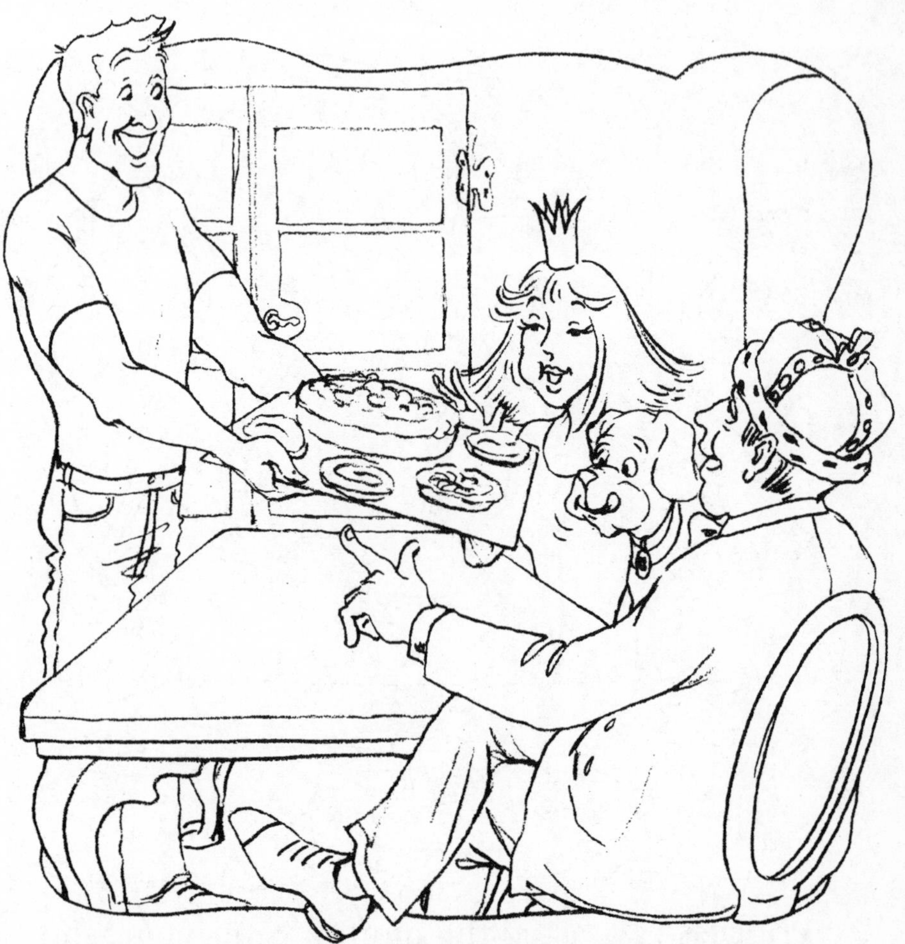

"Are you a prince?" asked King Raymund.

"I am not, but just taste," Jake said to Fay, and handed her his tray.

Princess Fay tasted the tart. "This lemon tart is the best," she said.

"Are things going well?" asked King Raymund.

"Not well at all," said Princess Fay. "Not one of them can bake cakes or make tarts."

"I can," said Jake. "Just let me have a chance."

"Help Princess Fay!" King Raymund exclaimed. "She wishes to wed a prince who can bake."

It was in all the papers and on TV.

"I can bake cakes," said a man named Jake to his mom, "and my lemon tart is terrific."

But there was no cake that met Princess Fay's standards. She could not recall when she tasted worse cake.

Princess Fay and Cupcake tasted and retasted.

"But you are not a prince," said Jake's mom. "You are fit to dig wells, not to wed a princess and bake cakes with her."

"But I bake better cakes," said Jake.

"Go rebuild a fence," said his mom.

"I'd rather make lemon tarts," Jake said.

Jake did not rebuild the fence. He made his best cake, his terrific lemon tart, and his best muffins. Then he went to stand with the princes at the gate. They waited and waited for Princess Fay.

The Contest

"Let's start," said King Raymund to the first prince.

"My dog Cupcake and I will act as tasters. We will taste and retaste," Princess Fay said. "If you can bake cakes and make tarts, we will wed."

Dear Mom,

Please do not pick me up in a week.

The city is pretty, but I like the farm, too.

Hugs and Kisses,

Eve

This is my Kitten, Fuzzy.

City Girl

by Dennis Anderson

illustrated by Meryl Henderson

Letter for Eve 3

Letter from Eve 12

Book 14

A Division of The McGraw-Hill Companies

Columbus, Ohio

SRA OPEN COURT READING

www.sra4kids.com

SRA/McGraw-Hill

A Division of The **McGraw·Hill** *Companies*

Printed in the United States of America.

Send all inquiries to:
SRA/McGraw-Hill
8787 Orion Place
Columbus, OH 43240-4027

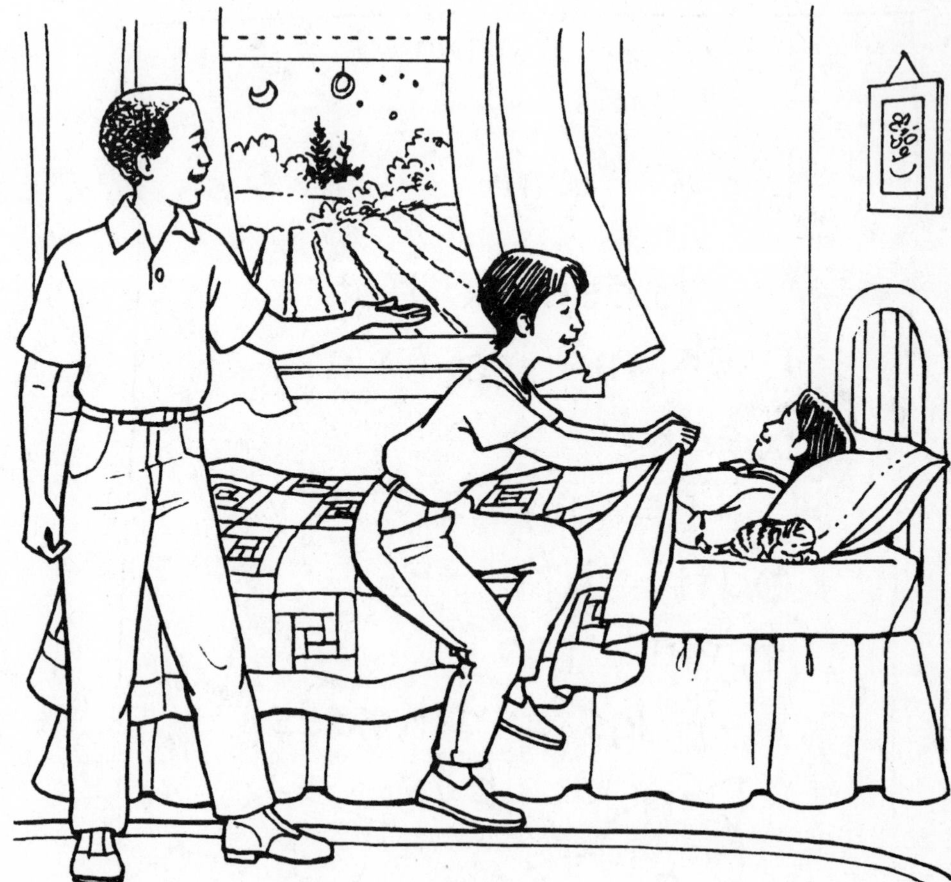

Lee tucked Eve into bed.

"From your bed, you can see the sleepy farm," said Steve.

"I'm tired, too—like my kitten," Eve said sleepily.

"Sweet dreams, farm girl," Lee whispered.

"Shhh!" whispered Steve. "See the deer leaping?"
"Deer do not leap in the city!" said Eve.

SRA Open Court Reading

Letter for Eve

One day, Eve received a letter.

"A letter for me?" said Eve. "Maybe it's about a party!"

Dear Eve,

We miss you.

Please come and visit us on our farm.

Hugs and kisses,

Steve and Lee

"What is it?" asked Eve.

"Little bugs," said Lee. "Each bug has a little beam that is twinkling on and off."

Letter from Eve

"Here you are! The farm is busy in the day, and it's busy after dark, too, Eve. Come on and see!"

"But I can't leave the city, Mommy!" Eve complained. "We really have fun here!"

Eve's mom tried to make her feel better. "You'll have fun going to Steve and Lee's farm, too. You'll see, sweetie."

Eve still was not sure she wanted to visit the farm.

"I'll eat a piece of yummy candy. Then I'll feel better," Eve whispered to herself.

But eating the candy did not make Eve feel better. She still was not sure about visiting the farm.

"Eve, I can hear that you are tired," Mom said gently. "I'll pick you up in a week, sweetie."

"Mom, it's muddy and dirty and dusty here! The geese are mean! Please come and get me. Steve and Lee can come to our home!"

Steve and Lee met Eve at the train.

"We are very happy you are here!" beamed Steve.

"You are a city girl now. But you can be a farm girl, too," added Lee.

"I'm happy being a city girl," said Eve. "I am not sure about being a farm girl!"

"This is our farm," said Steve happily.

"Let's feed these geese," said Steve.

Eve peeked at the geese. "I do not like geese," she whispered.

"Arf, Arf," said Pooch.

Drip, drip, splash, splash went the water.

"Let's eat!" said Walter. And he didn't worry over his silver ever again.

SRA OPEN COURT READING

SRA OPEN COURT READING

The Prince's Foolish Wish

by Laura Edwards
illustrated by Linda Kelen

The Prince and the Worm 3
The Foolish Wish 10

Book 15

A Division of The McGraw-Hill Companies
Columbus, Ohio

SRA OPEN COURT READING

www.sra4kids.com
SRA/McGraw-Hill
A Division of The McGraw-Hill Companies

Printed in the United States of America.

Send all inquiries to:
SRA/McGraw-Hill
8787 Orion Place
Columbus, OH 43240-4027

This time Walter was careful. He stopped to think. Then he said, "I wish that everything would return to the way it was."

"Commendable. Your wish is granted, and you have had a good education," said the worm.

"Oh, worm, you were right. I made a foolish wish. I can't eat. I turned poor Pooch to silver. I want to eat. I want Pooch to be furry again. I want to return to the way I was."

"You have just one more wish," said the worm. "Do you want to eat? Do you want Pooch back? Try to be wise. Do not make an unwise wish."

The Prince and the Worm

Walter was a selfish prince. He liked only two things. He liked his dog, Pooch, and he liked silver. He had piles and piles of silver. Each night he would lock his treasure room. Each morning he would unlock his treasure room. Then he would stack and restack the piles of silver.

One day Walter was playing with Pooch in the garden. The sunlight sparkled on the water in the pool. This made Walter wonder, "Wouldn't it be wonderful if the pool were filled with silver?"

All of a sudden, Walter heard a splash. He spotted a little worm in the water. He lifted the worm from the pool. Walter was ready to toss the worm away. Suddenly it spoke.

"Pooch! Poor Pooch! Worm! Worm! I need you!" cried Walter.

The little worm poked its head out of the earth. "How can a worthless worm help a wealthy prince?" asked the worm.

Walter returned to the garden. Pooch had a bone.

"Look, Pooch," said Walter. "We can play with a silver bone."

Walter picked up the bone. It turned to silver. He tossed the bone across the path. Pooch fetched the bone and returned to Walter.

"Nice dog, Pooch," said Walter. He bent over to pet Pooch on the head. In an instant, Pooch froze. Instantly, Pooch turned to silver!

"Don't throw me away," said the worm.

"Why not?" asked Walter. "What is a little worm worth to me?"

The worm said, "I am not worthless. I'm a magic worm. I can grant you three wishes. What do you want? Use your imagination."

"I would like my pool filled with silver," said Walter.

"So it is," said the worm.

When the pool filled with silver, Walter was unable to speak. "I am speechless," he said to the worm.

"You have two more wishes," said the worm. "But I must warn you to take care. Be careful what you wish."

Walter heard only the words *two more wishes.* The worm's warning was unheard. Walter's reaction was quick.

But Walter soon discovered his first problem. Each bite he tried to eat turned to silver. He was unable to eat anything. Soon he had a plate of uneaten silver food. He felt much discomfort.

The Foolish Wish

Walter rushed into his palace. He put his hand on each thing he spied. Soon he had silver carpets, silver tables, and a silver throne.

"I'm hungry," said Walter. "I will have lunch, then I will spend all afternoon turning things to silver."

"I wish that everything I touch would turn to silver," said Walter.

"That is not a good situation," said the worm.

"Your job is to grant my wish," said Walter. "You heard what I want."

"Your wish is granted," said the worm. "Perhaps you will learn a lesson. Only a fool makes foolish wishes."

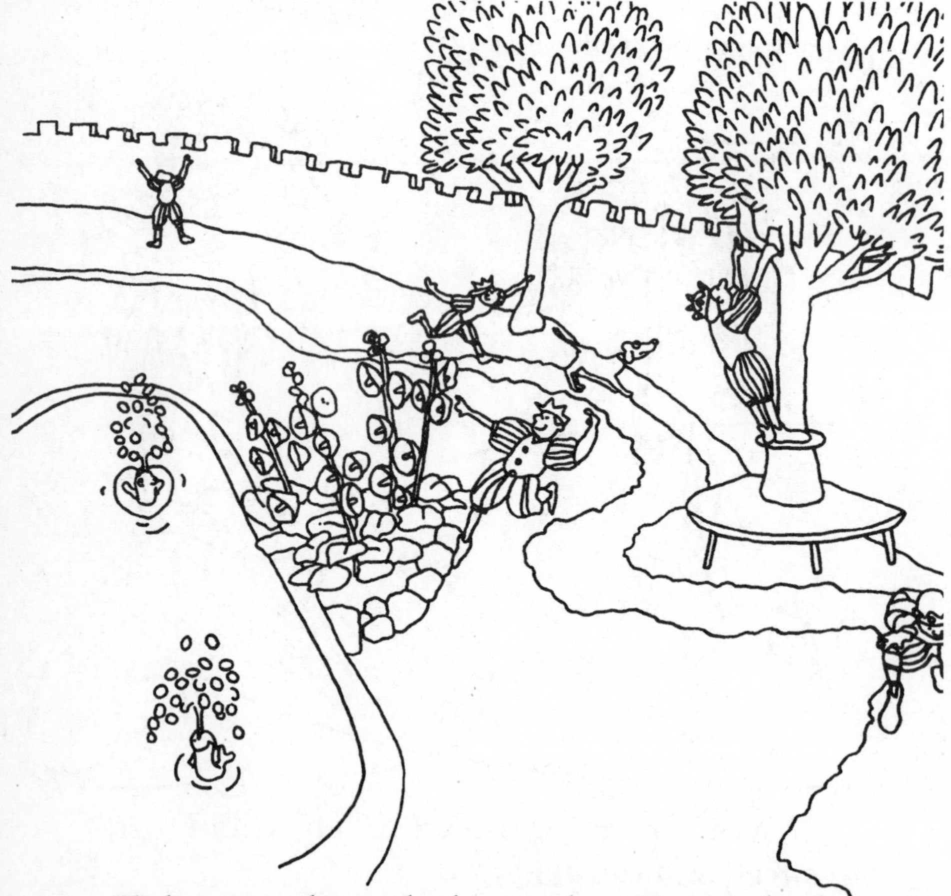

Walter ran through the garden. He touched chairs, the roses, and the stones on the path. Everything turned to silver.

"It works! It works!" cried Walter. "Watch this!" He put his hand under the water. Clink, clink, clink! He heard the silver drip into a pile.

"Yes, it works," said the worm. "I will dig into the soft earth. That is where I will be when you need me."

"I won't need you," snapped Walter. "I have all the wealth I need. A wealthy prince does not need a worthless little worm."

"Maybe you were frightened, but you were brave as well," said the king. "You faced a fear, and that is very brave. You really are Rose the Brave."

Rose smiled and struck her bold pose.

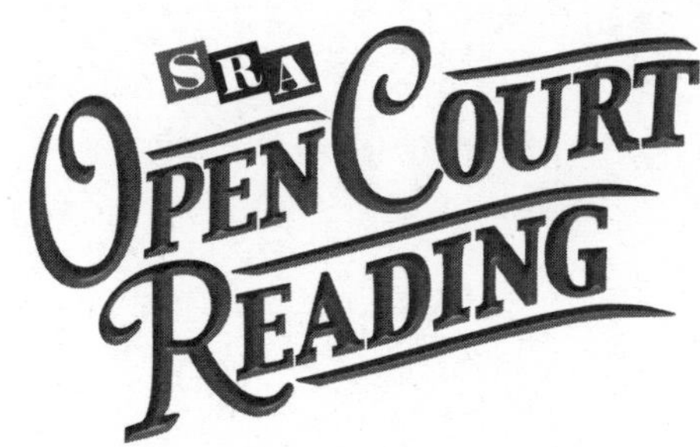

Rose the Brave

by Lisa Trumbauer
illustrated by Kersti Frigell

Rose Is Not Afraid 3
Rose Faces Her Fear 10

Book 16

A Division of The McGraw-Hill Companies
Columbus, Ohio

www.sra4kids.com
SRA/McGraw-Hill
A Division of The **McGraw·Hill** *Companies*

Printed in the United States of America.

Send all inquiries to:
SRA/McGraw-Hill
8787 Orion Place
Columbus, OH 43240-4027

The king was angry, but very glad, when Rose got home.

"I told you not to go into the forest alone," he scolded Rose. "You are lucky you were not hurt."

"I know," said Rose, "but I had to show that I was brave. I will never go into the forest by myself again."

Then Rose told the tale of her day. When she got to the end, she said, "I was not so brave after all. In fact, I was very frightened."

So Rose left the doe, the goat, and the toad to go home.

Rose did not want to admit that she had not acted as bravely as her boast. But she could not delay any longer. The king would be very upset that she went into the forest by herself.

Rose Is Not Afraid

Rose was a princess. But she was not an average princess.

Rose boasted that nothing could scare her. She was very brave.

"I am Rose the Brave!" she would say.

But no one ever believed Rose.

"You just sit on a throne all day. You don't have to be brave to do that," they said.

"Fine," said Rose to herself, "I will just show them that I am as brave as I boast. I will row my boat to the far shore of the moat and show that I am very brave."

"Thank you so much," said Rose. "I am sorry I ran when you spoke to me," she added. "I was frightened of you."

"It's okay," said the animals. "We are glad we could help. And you don't have to be frightened of us anymore."

One by one the three animals appeared, and Rose told them how she fell in the hole.

"We will help you," said the doe.

"Yes, I know just what to do," said the goat.

"You don't need to be frightened anymore," added the toad.

The doe got a rope, and the goat made a bow.

Then the toad let the rope go for Rose to climb up.

Rose rowed her boat to the far shore easily.

But when she reached the shore, she was still not happy.

"That was not scary at all," she said. "I need to do something really brave."

"I know," Rose said to herself, "I will go into the forest and show that I am really brave."

So Rose roamed the forest. The birds chirped, and animals ran near her path.

"This is not scary," Rose said. "How will I show that I am brave?"

Suddenly a voice said, "Hello!"

"Who's there?" Rose asked.

"I am a doe," came the reply.

Rose had never known a speaking doe before. Rose felt frightened, and so she ran.

"I must get help," Rose said to herself. "I will wipe my tears and try not to be frightened of the strange speaking animals."

"Hello, doe! Hello, goat! Hello, toad!" yelled Rose. "I am stuck in a hole, and I need help."

Rose Faces Her Fear

"What will I do?" Rose asked herself.

"I am not really Rose the Brave. I ran when the doe, the goat, and the toad spoke to me. I was frightened."

Rose began to cry.

"I am all by myself, stuck in a hole, and I am very frightened."

Rose could not run anymore, so she sat on a large stone. She was upset that she had run when the doe spoke.

"I was not frightened," she told herself, "I was just shocked. I am Rose the Brave."

"Hello, Rose the Brave," said a voice.

"Who's there?" Rose asked.

"I am a goat," came the reply.

Rose had never known a speaking goat before. Rose felt frightened, and so she ran.

"This is silly," said Rose to herself. "I am not frightened of a doe and a goat!" Rose struck a bold pose by a toad on a log and said, "I am Rose the Brave."

"Hello, Rose," said the toad. "It's nice to meet you. I am Joe the toad."

Rose had never seen a toad speak before. Rose felt frightened, and so she ran.

Rose ran and ran.
She ran until she hit her toe.
"Ouch," cried Rose, and she fell into a hole.
"Oh, no!"

"So, Joan, will you try it?" asked Hugo.

"No, thanks," said Joan. "I will simply use my phone."

SRA Open Court Reading

Hugo Bugle

by Dennis Fertig
illustrated by Robert Byrd

Toast 3
A New Unit 11

Book 17

A Division of The McGraw-Hill Companies
Columbus, Ohio

www.sra4kids.com

SRA/McGraw-Hill

A Division of The **McGraw-Hill** *Companies*

Printed in the United States of America.

Send all inquiries to:
SRA/McGraw-Hill
8787 Orion Place
Columbus, OH 43240-4027

“Wherever you go, you can easily use this unit. If you tie it on your chin, you can use it when you ride a bike, row a boat, or fly an airplane.”

"The code is made of blaring tones from bugle, flute, and tuba music. A spy will not have a clue to what you say. A spy will hear the happiest tune, not a clue."

Toast

"Spike, I have a new idea," said Hugo. "It is a fast, easy way to have hot—not cold—toast when you wake up."

"At night, tie a shiny pie plate to a wire. Make the wire go to a window. Set a bag of marbles by the window. By the bed, put a few stones."

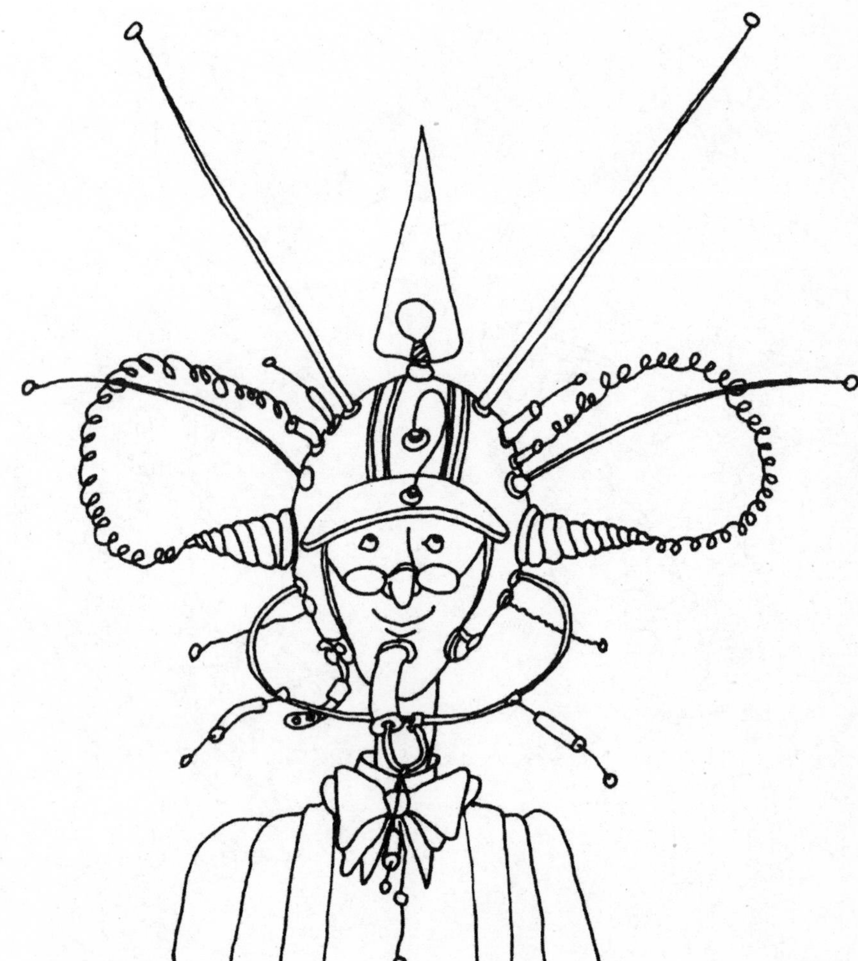

"Right on the top is a light in a red cone. While the light glows, it shows that a special microchip is in use. The microchip changes speech into code."

"The unit is a huge hat. It has wires, fuses, and tubes. Use the blue tube to speak. To hear, use the white tubes in the holes on the sides."

"Place a tube on the side of the window. Below the tube, glue the blue pail to the end of a pole. Put the pole under—not over—the lower window."

"Tie a rope to this side of the window. Tie a heavy ice cube tray to the rope. It must be heavy—not light. Load the toaster. Go to bed."

A New Unit

"Joan, you might like my new idea," said Hugo.

"I will try," said Joan with a rosy smile.

"It is a unit that you use to speak to anybody, even miles away," said Hugo.

"Tell me the truth, Spike. Is this a cool idea?" asked Hugo.

"Oh, my. The idea is nice," said Spike, "if you like toast. But I dislike toast."

SRA Open Court Reading

"Wake up to noisy music. Scoop some of the heavier stones into the shiny pie plate. When the shiny plate drops, the closed window opens."

"When the top window opens, sliding marbles go through the tube. The pail fills, and the pole dives low. Then the lower unopened window pops wide open."

"The heavy ice cube tray hits the right spot. And very soon, up pop the warmest slices of toast."

Queen Kit smiled sweetly.

SRA OPEN COURT READING

SRA OPEN COURT READING

Queen Kit

by Lisa Trumbauer
illustrated by Shawn McManus

Maybe This! 3
Surprise! 10

Book 18

A Division of The McGraw-Hill Companies
Columbus, Ohio

SRA OPEN COURT READING

www.sra4kids.com

SRA/McGraw-Hill

A Division of The **McGraw·Hill** *Companies*

Printed in the United States of America.

Send all inquiries to:
SRA/McGraw-Hill
8787 Orion Place
Columbus, OH 43240-4027

And the tasty bite spilled.
It spilled on Queen Kit
who looked surprised.
And what do you think
Queen Kit did?

"Surprise!" said Conrad.
"This tasty bite
will be a treat to eat!"
But Conrad tripped
on his own two feet.

Maybe This!

Queen Kit sat in her seat.
She sat glumly with her chin on her hand.
Queen Kit did not smile.
It was hard to rule the nation.

The queen was not mean.
The queen was just glum.
"What can we do to make Queen Kit smile?"
her subjects asked each other.

"Surprise!" said Tom.
"This flying kite is just right, Queen Kit!"
But Tom let it go.
And the kite got away.
That was not his intention.

"Surprise!" said Pete.
"This purring pet is perfect!"
But Pete dropped the pet.
And the pet ran away.
Pete was so upset.

"Maybe a cute dress that is easy to press will get a reaction.

It will please Queen Kit!" said Nell, the dressmaker.

"Maybe a quietly purring pet from my collection will please Queen Kit!" said Pete, the pet seller.

But Nell tripped on the dress and fell, letting out a little yell.

Surprise!

"Surprise!" said Nell, the dressmaker.

"The cut of this cute dress will make you feel better. It is my creation for you."

"Maybe a flying kite that shines brightly will help the situation," said Tom, the toy maker.

"Maybe a tasty bite to eat
that is not too sweet
will please Queen Kit!"
said Conrad, the cook.

"We will surprise the queen!" said the men.
So they hid the cute dress, the purring pet, the flying kite, and the tasty bite to eat.

Unlike dodoes, bald eagles did not become extinct. Perhaps we learned from the dodo. Perhaps in its own way the dodo saved the bald eagle.

Dead as a Dodo, Bald as an Eagle

by Ellen Garin
illustrated by Pat Lucas-Morris

Dead as a Dodo..........................3
Bald as an Eagle 10

Book 19

A Division of The McGraw-Hill Companies
Columbus, Ohio

SRA Open Court Reading

www.sra4kids.com

SRA/McGraw-Hill

A Division of The ***McGraw-Hill*** *Companies*

Printed in the United States of America.

Send all inquiries to:
SRA/McGraw-Hill
8787 Orion Place
Columbus, OH 43240-4027

That help came just in time for eagles. There are still not as many bald eagles as before, but things are better. We are learning to care for bald eagles as well as other animals. We are learning to share Earth.

Bald eagles were in trouble, just like dodoes had been. But this time, Americans decided to help. Laws were passed that protected eagle nesting lands. In 1972, the United States stopped using bug spray that hurt eagles.

SRA OPEN COURT READING

Dead as a Dodo

The stories of the dodo and the bald eagle begin in the same way but have very different endings—one sad and one happy. Read on to see how the story of one bird showed us ways to help the other.

Do you know this saying: "Dead as a dodo"? Do you know what it means?

The dodo was a bird that once lived, but is now extinct. *Extinct* means that there are no more. They have all died.

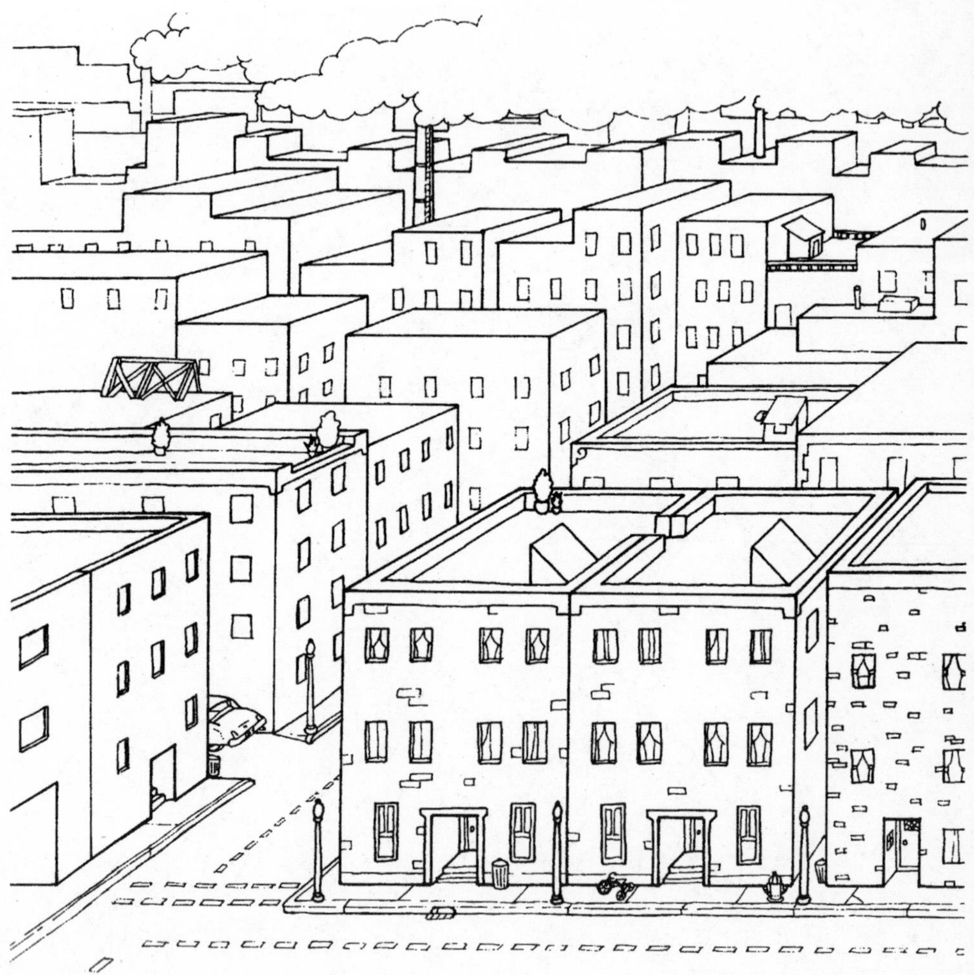

More than bug spray harmed bald eagles. Many eagles lost nests when people cleared land for homes and factories. Eagles had fewer places to live. Just like dodoes, bald eagles began dying.

In the 1940s, farmers began using a new spray to help get rid of bugs that ruin crops. This spray hurt bald eagles as well as other birds and animals. After being near this spray, many bald eagles could not lay eggs. Those that could, laid eggs with thin shells that cracked before the chicks were ready to hatch. Bald eagles were in trouble.

The dodo was about the size of a turkey. It had a large hooked beak, small wings, and a heavy body with fat yellow legs. The dodo was a bird, but it was unable to fly. It lived in forests on an island in the Indian Ocean.

The story of how the dodo became extinct starts on an island near Africa. It is a place with rich soil and lush plants.

The bald eagle has a brown body with a white head and tail. Its beak, eyes, and feet are yellow. Perhaps you know the saying "Bald as an eagle." The bald eagle is not really bald. It got its name from its white head. Unlike dodoes, bald eagles are strong fliers and lay eggs in trees or on high cliffs. Bald eagles live only in North America.

Bald as an Eagle

Have you ever seen pictures of bald eagles? Most likely, you have. The bald eagle has been the United States's bird since 1782. Its picture is on dollar bills we use every day.

When Dutch settlers landed on the island in 1598, there were many dodoes living there.

By 1681, less than one hundred years after Dutch settlers first landed, every dodo had died.

Dodoes built nests on the land but not in trees. When settlers came, they had dogs and wild pigs with them. Pigs and dogs raided dodo nests and ate the eggs. Dodoes laid only one egg at a time, so their eggs were quickly eaten.

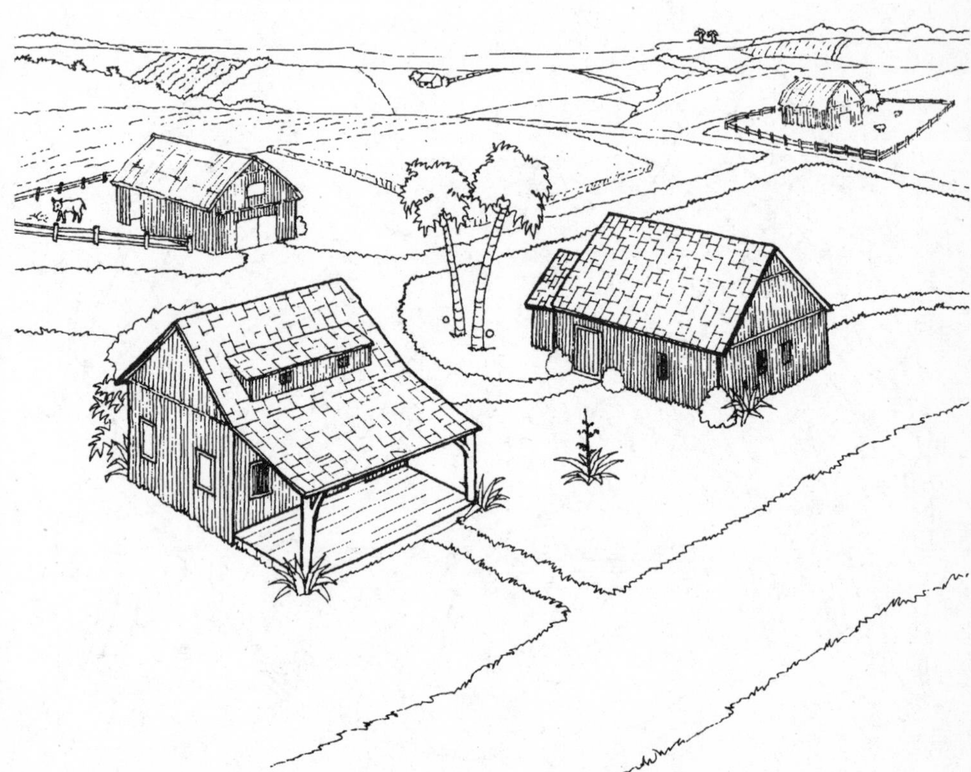

Settlers cleared land for homes and farms. This left dodoes less room for nesting. Dodoes started dying, and before long they had vanished. That is why we say "Dead as a dodo." It means vanished, or extinct.

"Here, little turtle, swim hard," said Carlos. "You have a long way to go. Stay safe. Please come back to our scenic beach."

Scientists say that turtles have lived in the seas for many, many years. Turtles swam in the seas when dinosaurs lived.

The Lives of Sea Turtles

by Chris Meramec
illustrated by Diane Blasius

Turtles in the Sea 3
Baby Turtles 10

Book 20

A Division of The McGraw·Hill Companies
Columbus, Ohio

SRA OPEN COURT READING

www.sra4kids.com

SRA/McGraw-Hill

A Division of The **McGraw·Hill** *Companies*

Printed in the United States of America.

Send all inquiries to:
SRA/McGraw-Hill
8787 Orion Place
Columbus, OH 43240-4027

"We will never see them again," said Carlos.

"Yes, you may," said Papa. "Green sea turtles travel to faraway places like some birds do. But they come back to the beach where they were born to lay their eggs. These turtles will come back to this same beach for as long as they live."

"What will happen to the baby turtles?" asked Carlos.

"When they get to the sea, the little turtles will swim as hard as they can for two days. They will not even stop to eat. They may swim as far as Africa," said Papa.

Turtles in the Sea

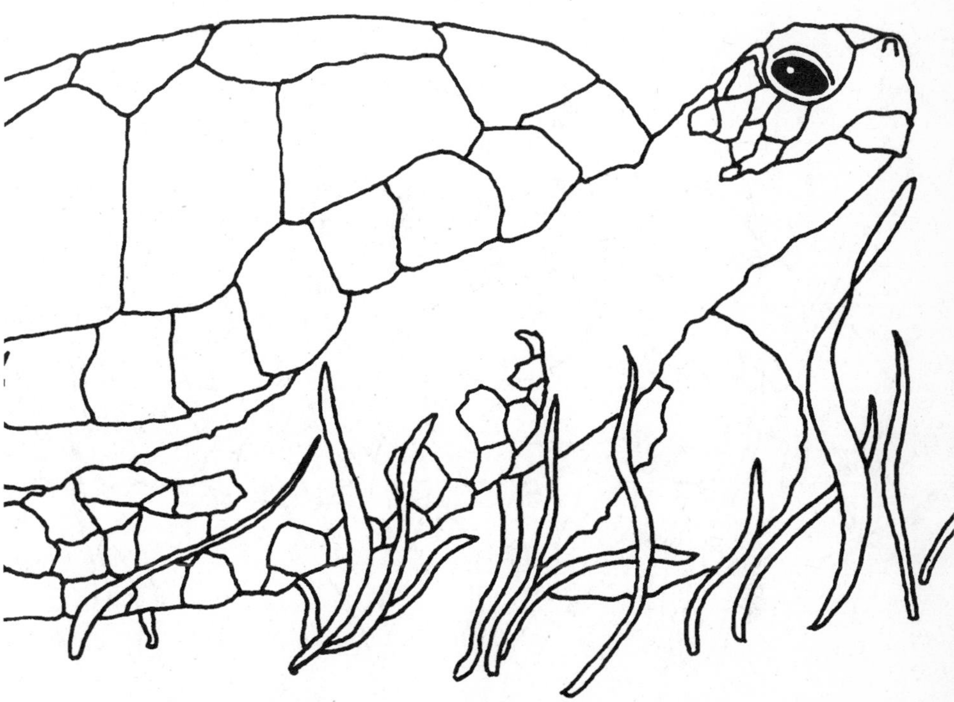

This is a green sea turtle. A sea turtle has flippers for feet. It flaps its flippers like wings when it swims. A sea turtle has a shell that makes swimming easy. The curved top and flat bottom help to lift the shell, and the turtle can glide through the sea.

The shell keeps the turtle safe from danger, too. But a sea turtle cannot pull in its head and legs. The sea turtle has a very thick skin and scales on its head and legs.

"Their little shells are so soft," said Carlos.

"Their shells will get harder as the turtles get bigger," said Papa.

"Go away," said Carlos. He waved his arms like scissors at the flying gulls.

"Even then they may not be safe," said Papa. "Big fish eat the soft little turtles, too."

"What a scene! There are hundreds and hundreds of little turtles!" said Carlos. "See, they are creeping to the sea."

"The little turtles try to get to the sea," said Papa. "But it is a hard trip. Their flippers are made for swimming, not for creeping on land."

Sea turtles eat and sleep in the sea. The green sea turtle eats tender sea grass that lies on the sandy bottom. It swims to the top to breathe.

Turtles do not have teeth, but they do have strong beaks. The beak of a sea turtle can crack shells. Sea turtles might eat shellfish, jellyfish, small sea animals, and wild sea plants.

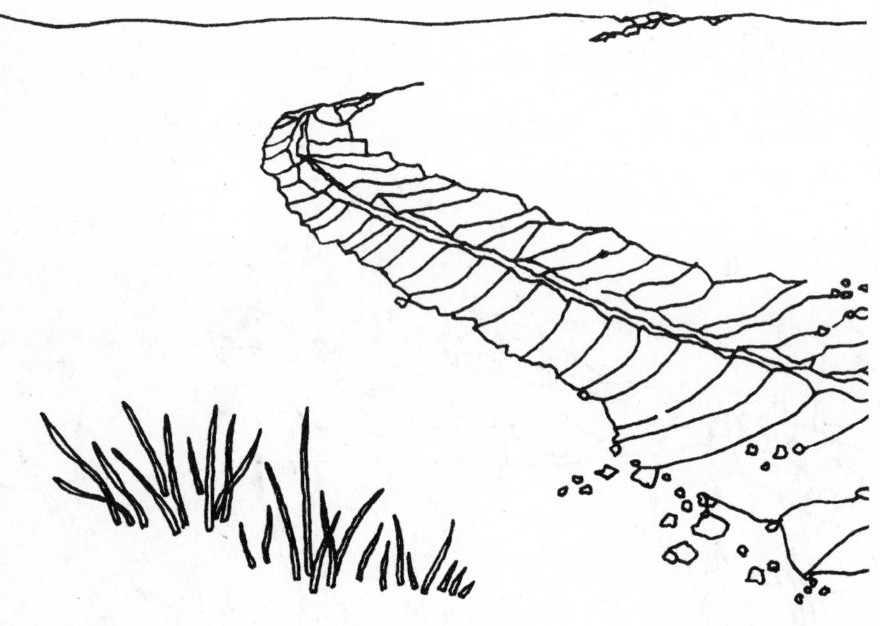

Sea turtles only leave the sea to lay their eggs. A mother turtle digs a nest in the sand. She lays hundreds of eggs in a pile. Then she covers the nest and returns to the sea. The sun keeps the sand and the eggs warm and dry. Mother turtles never see their babies.

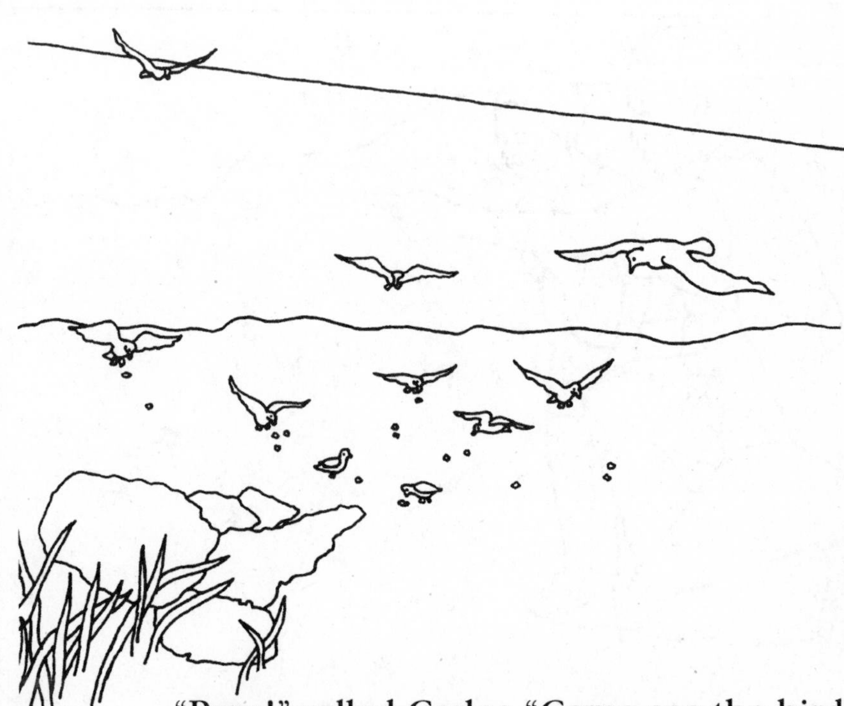

"Papa!" yelled Carlos. "Come see the birds. They are everywhere on the beach!"

"Turtle eggs must be hatching," said Papa. "The birds are feasting on baby turtles."

"Baby turtles! Let's hike down there!" said Carlos.

SRA OPEN COURT READING

Baby Turtles

When the eggs hatch, the shells of the baby turtles are soft. The little turtles must get to the sea. They start to edge across the sand. Danger awaits. Birds circle high in the sky. They eat many of the little turtles. Crabs eat some, too.

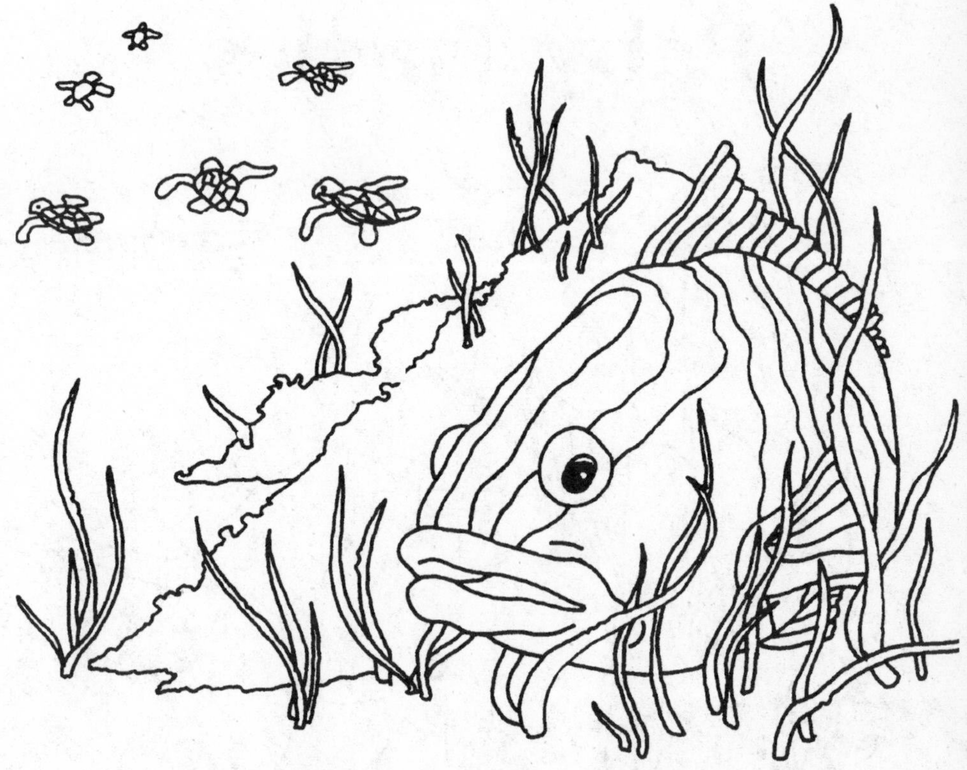

The baby turtles can swim when they are born. They can even find things to eat. But they are still not safe. Big fish hunt the soft little turtles.

Hundreds of turtles hatch on the beach. Many will be eaten. Not many will live to be big turtles.

At some time they will return to this same beach to lay their eggs.

Fairy Prion

This bird digs its own home and then gets an uninvited roommate. The tuatara, a prehistoric spiny reptile, shares the nest. During the day, the prion looks for food and the tuatara sleeps. Then at night, the prion returns and the tuatara goes hunting.

As you have read, birds provide many styles of homes—from nests to burrows—for their young.

Nesting and Burrowing Birds

by Marilee Robin Burton
illustrated by Meryl Henderson

Nests of All Kinds 3
Which Birds Burrow? 10

Book 21

A Division of The McGraw-Hill Companies
Columbus, Ohio

SRA OPEN COURT READING

www.sra4kids.com

SRA/McGraw-Hill

A Division of The **McGraw·Hill** *Companies*

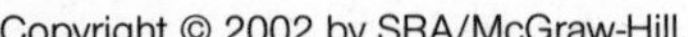

Printed in the United States of America.

Send all inquiries to:
SRA/McGraw-Hill
8787 Orion Place
Columbus, OH 43240-4027

Kookaburra

The kookaburra, well known for its jungle laugh, nests inside termite homes. It pecks a hole in the termite nest and burrows inside. But the termites don't leave. The bugs build a wall to block the bird's nest.

Crab-Loving Plover

The crab-loving plover is very unusual. It is the only shorebird that nests underground. These birds live in large flocks and make tunnel homes in sandy spots near the sea where crabs are plentiful.

Nests of All Kinds

There is at least one way that all birds are the same: they lay eggs. To keep the eggs and nestlings safe, most birds make nests. When making nests, however, birds display different skills and styles.

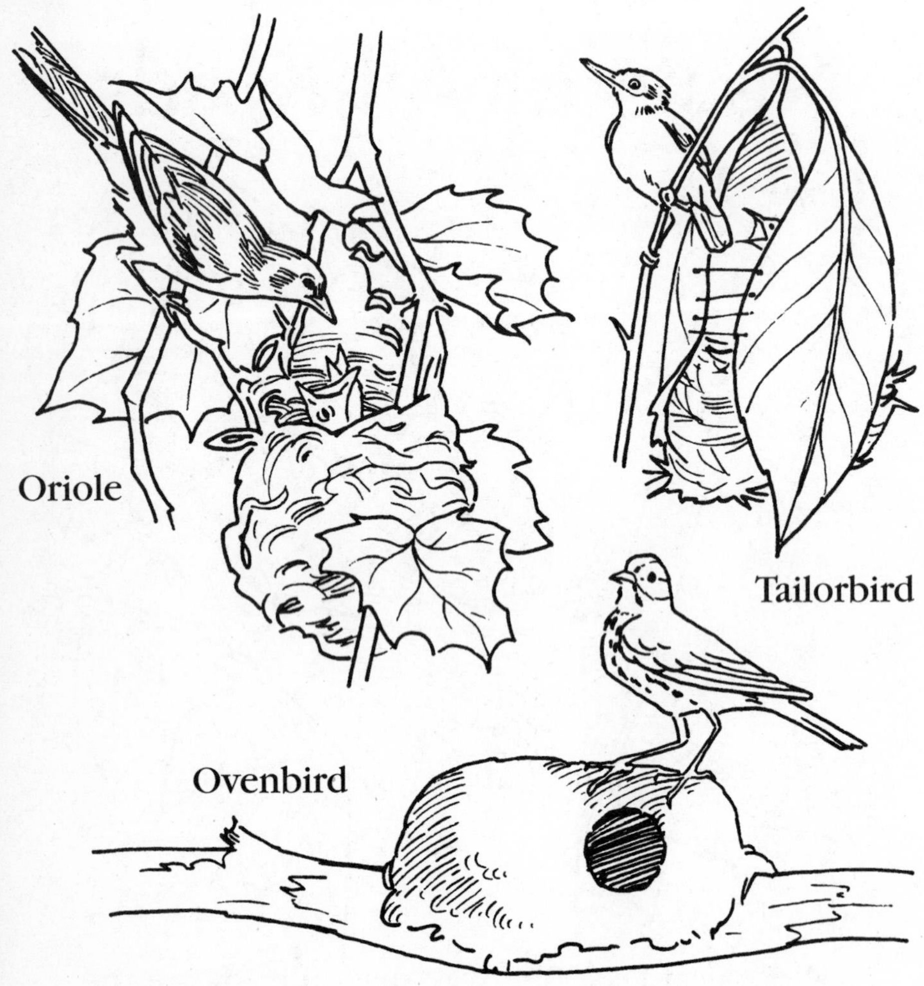

When it is time to make their own nests, most adult birds return to the place where they hatched. Every bird makes the same kind of nest that its parents made.

Kakapo Parrot

The kakapo is the biggest of all parrots. It's a flightless bird and spends its time on the ground. When it's nesting, it looks for holes near tree roots.

Elf Owl

The elf owl also likes to make its home in deserted holes. A tunnel drilled in a cactus by a woodpecker makes a perfect nest for this tiny owl.

A lot goes on in nest making. Beaks lift, weave, and drill. Feet stamp and dig! The process may look disorganized, but it isn't. The nests are very carefully constructed.

We normally think of nests as being in trees. But some aren't. Some birds make nests on rocky cliffs, sandy shores, in the water, and even underground!

Burrowing Owls

These birds live in treeless grassland. They can dig their own tunnels but prefer to take over someone else's. A prairie dog's unwanted home is ideal. If the size isn't exactly right, the owl simply enlarges it. It uses its feet to kick dirt and rubble backward out of the hole.

Which Birds Burrow?

Bee-Eaters

These small, bright birds make holes in riverbanks and cliffs. The common bee-eater repeatedly hurls itself headfirst into the dirt until it makes a dent. Then it stands in the dent and keeps digging to make a deeper tunnel.

Surprisingly, quite a few birds are burrow diggers! They make holes for their nests in trees, logs, cactus plants, and even in the dirt.

Some birds use the unwanted homes of other animals for their nests. They take over the empty den of a rabbit, skunk, or badger.

On the following pages you'll meet just a few of these fascinating birds.

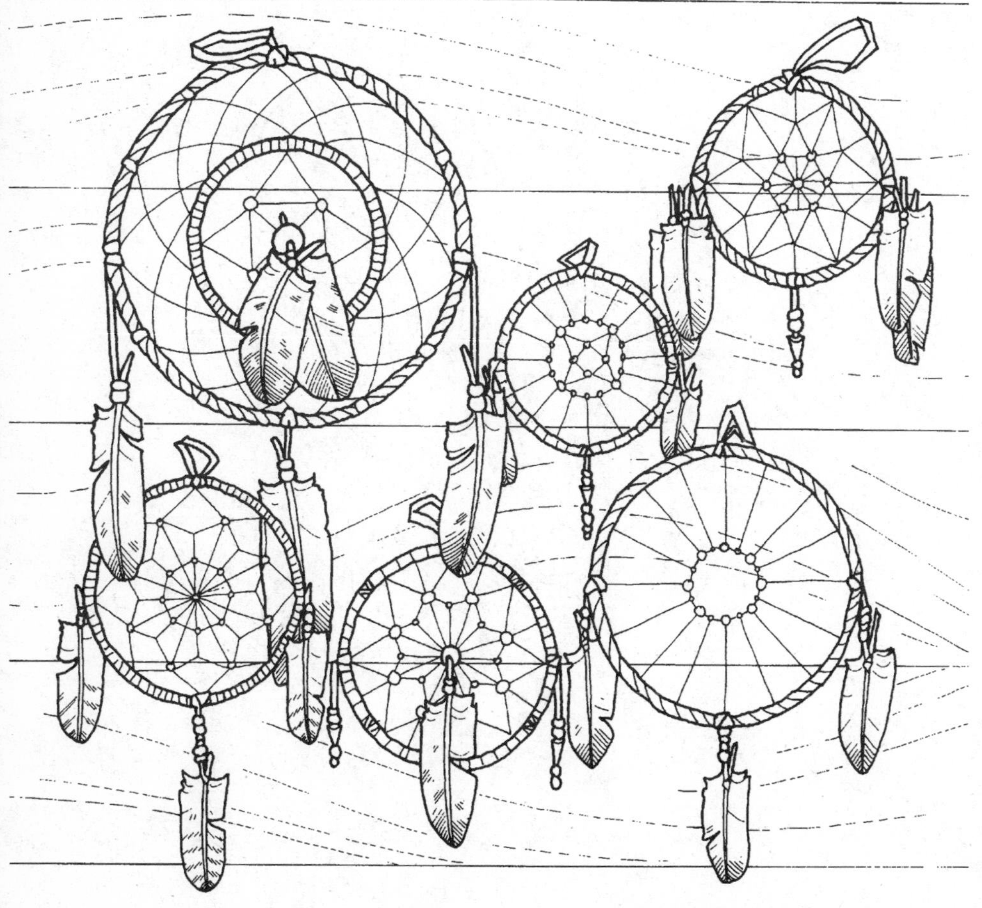

The children looked at their finished dreamcatchers. "Now you have your own dreamcatchers to hang. Next time you visit, you can share your good dreams with me," said Granddad Scott.

SRA Open Court Reading

Loop and Hook a Dream

by Phillip Ward
illustrated by Pat Lucas-Morris

Granddad Scott Tells Good Tales.....3
Look! A Dreamcatcher! 12

Book 22

A Division of The McGraw-Hill Companies
Columbus, Ohio

SRA Open Court Reading

www.sra4kids.com

SRA/McGraw-Hill

A Division of The **McGraw-Hill** *Companies*

Printed in the United States of America.

Send all inquiries to:
SRA/McGraw-Hill
8787 Orion Place
Columbus, OH 43240-4027

"Tie a feather to the end of a string, then thread the string with beads. Hook the loose string to the loop. You have made a dreamcatcher! Finally, add a loop so you can hang your dreamcatcher."

"Wrap your hoop with cloth. You can choose red, yellow, green, blue, or purple string to loop a web. Soon it will look like the spokes on a bicycle wheel."

Granddad Scott Tells Good Tales

The teacher took the children on a field trip to see Granddad Scott, the storyteller. The children sat on the wood floor. Granddad Scott stood in front of the children as he began to tell his colorful tales of dreams and dreamcatchers.

"When I was a boy, I knew a man named Running Brook. He made dreamcatchers by weaving yarn on hoops. I liked sitting with him while he worked because he told tales of his dreams."

"You can hook the beads and feathers any way you like, too! Just remember to leave a hole in the center."

Look! A Dreamcatcher!

Granddad Scott asked, "Do you want to make a dreamcatcher? You can loop the hoop your very own way."

From a nook in the wall, Granddad took down a strange-looking thing.

"Running Brook made this dreamcatcher for me out of string, beads, and feathers. He always made something special to share."

Granddad Scott shook his dreamcatcher high in the air. He pointed out that the dreamcatcher is like a spiderweb. It is a perfect circle with a hole in the center.

"Mr. Raccoon stops by and says, 'I'd like to share my lunch with you, Goose Skiddoo.' Goose Skiddoo thanks Mr. Raccoon for his good food. Then she calls to Hooting Owl, 'Please have noodles with us at noon.'"

The children laughed about this silly dream.

The second dream Granddad Scott told was a silly one. "Goose Skiddoo is in the doorway of her house. She flaps her wings and stoops low. Then she clears her throat and sings, 'Yellow, blue, red, and green! What can it all mean?'"

"Running Brook told me the bad dreams get caught and tangled in the web part of the dreamcatcher. The good dreams will go through the hole in the center," said Granddad Scott.

"Running Brook said that some people hang a dreamcatcher above their beds to sort through the good and bad dreams. The bad dreams are snared in the web. The good dreams slip through the hole and float down the beads and feathers. Only the good dreams land on the dreamer's head to be remembered."

Granddad Scott then shared two of his dreams with the children. "In one dream, Hooting Owl says, as he swoops to his tree, 'Be brave and not a fool. Look in books for proof.'"

Granddad Scott explained that this dream had a lesson. That is why he remembers it.

We never decided who put the pepper in Grandpa's soup. We didn't care. We sipped and swallowed every spoonful of Grandma's sweet and sour vegetable and dumpling soup.

Sweet and Sour Soup

by Phillip Ward
illustrated by Kersti Frigell

Grandpa's Sweet and Sour Soup 3
Waiting for Grandma's New Soup 8

Book 23

A Division of The McGraw-Hill Companies

Columbus, Ohio

SRA OPEN COURT READING

"Yum! Yum! Grandma, this soup is delicious. What is the secret of our house soup today?"

We all giggled and laughed loudly. Grandpa caught us by surprise! He liked Grandma's sweet and sour vegetable and dumpling soup!

www.sra4kids.com

SRA/McGraw-Hill

A Division of The McGraw-Hill Companies

Printed in the United States of America.

Send all inquiries to:
SRA/McGraw-Hill
8787 Orion Place
Columbus, OH 43240-4027

"Grandpa! We walked down by the pond and saw an owl, a cow, a fawn, and some pretty swans!"

Grandpa's Sweet and Sour Soup

"How did this happen? I know Grandpa does not allow pepper in his sweet and sour soup! It is our daughter's secret recipe."

A crowd gathered in the small kitchen.

"What shall we do now? How do we let Grandpa know that his sweet and sour soup has pepper in it?"

Grandma frowned and looked down at the kitchen floor. But then her eyebrows curved up as she smiled.

"I have it! I found the answer!"

Grandpa took another taste, then paused. "And there's not too much pepper!"

“What is this?” Grandpa took a sip of soup. “Sweet and sour vegetable and dumpling soup? I believe Grandma has found a new recipe! She ought to write this recipe down.”

“We will make Grandpa some sweet and sour vegetable and dumpling soup.”

"Grandma, what are those birds? They look like they are wearing lacy white gowns!"

Grandma knelt by the pond and laughed, "Swans are so pretty in their white feathery down. I wish we had brought some bread crumbs to feed them."

"Grandma! Listen! Hear the brown cow go 'Moo!' What a loud sound the brown cow makes. Look! It has frightened the fawn."

"We'll mix flour and water in a bowl to make dough. We'll knead the dough and roll it into little balls for dumplings. Then we'll add the dumplings and the vegetables to Grandpa's soup. It will be ready in an hour."

Waiting for Grandma's New Soup

"While our soup cooks, let's get some exercise and walk down by the pond. Maybe we'll see some animals. Maybe we'll see a swan or a fawn."

"Wow! Look, Grandma! What is that on the limb?"

Grandma replied softly, "It is a big brown owl, my dear. It has beautiful round eyes that can see in the dark."

"Look there! The brown cow is eating flowers!"

So Farmer Roy joined in the noisy song. When Joyce, Coil, and Lloyd saw Farmer Roy singing, they were filled with joy. One by one, all lifted their voices in song.

Joyce's happy "Mooooo," Coil's excited "Oink Oink," and Lloyd's loud "Cock-a-doodle-doo" mixed with Roy and the class in a very joyful song.

No Noise!

by Lisa Trumbauer
illustrated by Loretta Lustig

The Animals 3
The Children 10

Book 24

A Division of The McGraw-Hill Companies
Columbus, Ohio

SRA Open Court Reading

www.sra4kids.com

SRA/McGraw-Hill

A Division of The McGraw-Hill Companies

Printed in the United States of America.

Send all inquiries to:
SRA/McGraw-Hill
8787 Orion Place
Columbus, OH 43240-4027

The boys and girls lifted their voices in song.

But Joyce, Coil, and Lloyd stared at Farmer Roy and did not make a sound.

The class did not give up.

"You must join us, Farmer Roy," they said. "Lift your voice in song!"

"I am sorry," Farmer Roy said to the class. "I don't know why they won't make any noise."

The boys and girls looked on sadly.

"If we sing for them," the girls said, "maybe they will join us."

The Animals

The sun was bright, the flowers smelled sweet, and the birds were chirping out a song.

Joyce the cow was filled with so much joy that she felt like singing, too!

"I will lift my voice in song and dance a jig for joy!" said Joyce.

"Mooooo," sang Joyce as she went round and round.

Farmer Roy did not understand why Joyce and Coil did not make any noise.

"There is still the rooster," he told the class. "Maybe he will make some noise."

When they got to Lloyd, a boy stopped and pointed.

"Cock-a-doodle-doo!" said the boy.

But Lloyd made no noise. He was full of joy to share, but Farmer Roy had said, "No noise!"

Farmer Roy was surprised.

"Hmmm," he said. "Let's try visiting the pig."

When they got to Coil, a girl stopped and pointed.

"Oink Oink!" said the girl hopefully.

But Coil made no noise. He was full of joy to share, but Farmer Roy had said, "No noise!"

"Why are you singing?" asked Coil the pig.

"It's a great day! The sun is bright, the flowers smell sweet, and the birds are chirping out a song. I felt like singing, too," explained Joyce.

"Okay," said Coil. "Your joyful song has brought me delight. I will join you."

He did just that. Joyce's happy "Mooooo" mixed with Coil's excited "Oink Oink" in a noisy chord.

"Okay," said Farmer Roy. "You'll like my animals. They make lots of noise."

When they got to Joyce, a boy stopped and pointed.

"Moooo!" said the boy.

But Joyce stood quietly. She was full of joy to share, but Farmer Roy had said, "No noise!"

The Children

The next day, a class of boys and girls came to see Farmer Roy's farm. He showed them the barn, the fields, and all the machines, but they weren't satisfied.

"We want to see the cows and the pigs," said the girls.

"And I want to see a rooster," said a boy excitedly.

"Why are you singing?" asked Lloyd the rooster.

"The sun is shining brightly, the flowers smell sweet, and the birds are chirping out a joyful song. I felt like singing, too," explained Joyce.

"Okay," said Lloyd. "Your song of joy has filled me with delight! I will join you happily."

He did just that. Joyce's happy "Mooooo" mixed with Coil's excited "Oink Oink" and Lloyd's loud "Cock-a-doodle-doo" in a very noisy song.

"Stop that rowdy noise!" exclaimed Farmer Roy, who was getting annoyed. "There's too much work and too short a time for your silly songs. I don't want you to sing."

"It's good to be home. I like it much better than camping."

"It's much better than the beach, too."

Summer Pen Pals

by Dennis Anderson
illustrated by Meryl Henderson

It's Fun Here 3

It's Not So Much Fun Here 9

Book 25

A Division of The McGraw-Hill Companies

Columbus, Ohio

SRA OPEN COURT READING

www.sra4kids.com

SRA/McGraw-Hill

A Division of The McGraw-Hill Companies

Printed in the United States of America.

Send all inquiries to:
SRA/McGraw-Hill
8787 Orion Place
Columbus, OH 43240-4027

Dear Jan,

Each day here is warmer than the last.

I am tired of everything being hotter than hot.

I hope we go home soon, too.

That would be my choice.

Tammy

SRA Open Court Reading

It's Fun Here

Dear Tammy,

It's fun here at our campsite in the forest. It's as comfortable as our house.

There is so much more to do here than there is at home.

Yesterday, I waded in the lake.

Jan

Dear Jan,

I know what you mean.

There is always something fun to do.

Here at the beach we go swimming each day.

We have races to see who is the fastest swimmer.

I am the fastest swimmer in my family.

Tammy

Dear Tammy,

Can you believe it is still rainy here?

I am tired of everything being wetter than wet.

I can't wait to go home.

Mom caught a cold.

I will not leave sadly.

Jan

Hi, Jan.

We went fishing on a big boat today.

Mom and Dad both got sick, but I got even sicker.

It was awful.

We certainly won't do this daily.

Tammy

Hi, Tammy!

Last night we hiked in the dark. We had no backpacks. We brought a flashlight but didn't need it.

The moon looked so big.

A bat flapped near us.

Tim yelled, but I didn't! Mom and Dad joined us by the lake.

Jan

Hi, Jan!

We all like to go fishing on the dock before noontime.

Dad caught the littlest fish.

I caught the biggest!

We bought chips to eat with the fish.

Tammy

Hi, Tammy.

Hiking is no fun when it's raining.

The path was muddy, and it got muddier.

I fought to keep from falling. I got soaked and dirty.

It has hardly stopped raining all day.

Jan

Dear Jan,

It's not like that here.

Today is the hottest day since we got here.

I got badly sunburned, and it really hurts!

Now I have to stay inside until I am better.

Tammy

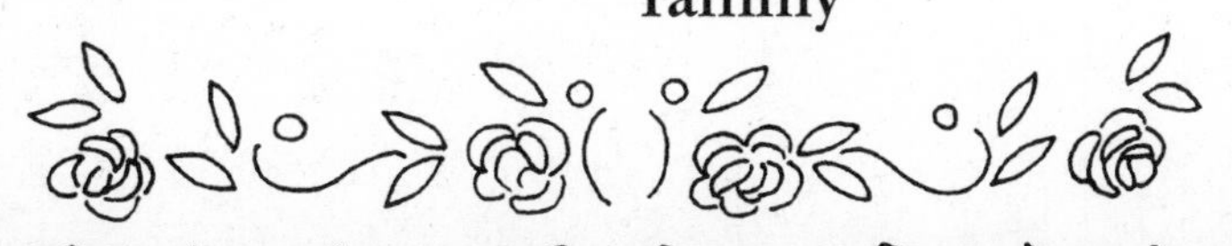

Tammy,

The kids here are awfully nice.

We play games and go for hikes. I taught them some new games.

They all go camping a lot, so they teach me cool things.

We formed some teams. Everyone can join.

Jan

Jan,

The kids here are nice, too.

We make sand castles, tell stories, and make lots of noise.

They are the funniest! I almost lost my voice from laughing.

I hardly miss home at all.

Tammy

It's Not So Much Fun Here

Dear Tammy,

Mom and I rowed on the lake.

It got colder and colder.

I still haven't warmed up. Brrr!

It is very quiet. I could use some noise.

Jan

"Your story was really good!" said Soo Lin.

"So was yours!" said Joyce. "We don't ever have to be afraid again … as long as we are in the same room and can help each other feel brave."

SRA OPEN COURT READING

Joyce Writes a Good Story

by Carolyn Crimi
illustrated by Meg McLean

A Good Idea....................................3
Joyce in Class...............................11

Book 26

A Division of The McGraw-Hill Companies
Columbus, Ohio

SRA OPEN COURT READING

www.sra4kids.com

SRA/McGraw-Hill

A Division of The McGraw-Hill Companies

Printed in the United States of America.

Send all inquiries to:
SRA/McGraw-Hill
8787 Orion Place
Columbus, OH 43240-4027

When Joyce stood up to read, her knees shook. She felt awful. She felt awkward. Then she looked at Soo Lin, who was smiling. Joyce felt better. She read her story, and the class applauded. No one disliked her story.

At school, Joyce talked to her friend Soo Lin. "I'm afraid to read my story out loud," she said to Soo Lin.

"Me, too!" said Soo Lin. "But I thought I was the only one who was afraid."

"I know!" Soo Lin went on. "I'll look at you, and you look at me when we read. Maybe that will prevent us from feeling scared."

SRA OPEN COURT READING

A Good Idea

Joyce had to write a story for school. She thought and thought, but she did not know what to write about.

"Why not write about a boy and his toys," said her brother.

Joyce disagreed. She really wanted to do better.

Joyce's sister said, "Why not write about a girl with brown hair and the prettiest voice ever?"

"That would not be my first choice," said Joyce.

Joyce caught the school bus. She saw Howard and Shawn.

"We know our stories by heart," said Shawn.

Joyce felt worse. She wanted to know her story by heart, too. She tried to prepare. She repeated her story over and over.

Joyce looked for her books. She took her time. She did not care if she was late. She was very uncomfortable.

Joyce's father was in the garden watering flowers. Joyce asked him what she should write about.

"You could write about a man and flowers prettier than anyone's," said her father.

"No," said Joyce. "That's not good. I want it to be the best."

Next door, Joyce saw Howard and Shawn playing football on the lawn.

"Have you finished your story?" asked Shawn.

"Not yet," said Joyce.

"You can't disobey," said Howard. "We must read them out loud tomorrow."

Joyce in Class

"I am afraid to read my story aloud to the class," said Joyce.

"Calm down," said Mom. "You won't make any mistakes. But hurry or you will miss the bus and have to ride your bicycle."

Joyce took out her notebook.

"What is your story about?" asked her sister.

"A girl who does not know what to write about," said Joyce.

"Am I in your story?" asked her sister.

"Of course! You are the second person in my story," said Joyce.

Joyce found Mom and sat down with a frown.

"Did you think of something to write about?" asked Mom.

Joyce shook her head.

"You should write about the things you know best," said Mom. "Then you will enjoy it."

Joyce went for a walk. She walked and talked to herself. She thought about what her mother had said. Suddenly, Joyce had her first good idea.

Joyce ran back to her house faster than a mouse. She ran past Howard and Shawn on the lawn. She ran past her father. She ran past her sister and her brother.

"Where's the fire?" asked Mom.

"In my head!" shouted Joyce with joy.

With a great roar, Lion jumped into the river. Little Hare stood by and watched from behind the tall grass. Then she quickly ran back to the village before Lion came out of the water.

When Little Hare returned to her village, she shared her news with the happy crowd. "Lion will not be able to find his way back to our village. We will never see that lion again."

Little Hare

by Tim Paulson
illustrated by Deborah Colvin Borgo

Old Hare's Plan.......................... 3
Little Hare's Plan 9

Book 27

A Division of The McGraw-Hill Companies
Columbus, Ohio

www.sra4kids.com

SRA/McGraw-Hill

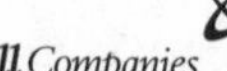

A Division of The McGraw-Hill Companies

Printed in the United States of America.

Send all inquiries to:
SRA/McGraw-Hill
8787 Orion Place
Columbus, OH 43240-4027

Lion roared, "So you robbed me of my meal! Come out of the water and fight!"

But the big lion stayed put.

"If you won't come out and fight," Lion growled, "I'll come in and get you." Lion bared his teeth and narrowed his eyes. So did the big lion.

Just then Little Hare began to hop up and down.

"Look!" she cried. "In the river! I see him!"

Lion raced to the riverbank and stared into the water.

Old Hare's Plan

Lion had a fierce appetite. No matter how much he ate, he was unsatisfied. Some told that Lion could eat fifty elephants and twenty giraffes and ten zebras at once—and then enjoy more.

Each day Lion raided an animal village and ate everything in sight. The animals were fearful.

Old Hare—the oldest and wisest animal—called an emergency meeting.

Old Hare cleared his throat, and the crowd fell silent.

"I have a plan," he began, "that will save our village and put an end to Lion."

"Almost there!" Little Hare sang out. "Just a little bit farther!" And still they walked, and still there was no big lion.

"I've had it!" cried Lion in disgust. "You have tricked me! There is no big lion. There is just me and you—and I am going to eat YOU right now!"

Lion and Little Hare walked for miles and miles. They crossed grasslands, plains, and marshes.

"Where is this big lion?" roared Lion. "I'm so hungry I could eat ten of him—and then have *you* for a snack!"

A great noise rose from the crowd. Old Hare called for silence.

"Each day," he continued, "one of us will go to Lion and offer to be eaten. Then Lion will leave the rest of us alone."

There were loud hurrays. But the animals were unwilling to volunteer.

Just then Little Hare piped up. "I will go," she said quietly.

"Three cheers for Little Hare!" cried the animals. "Farewell, farewell, brave Little Hare!" they called out. But really they thought she was foolish.

"I don't care HOW scary he is," boomed Lion. "Show him to me. How dare he eat my good dinner!"

"There were zebras, elephants, chimpanzees, and lots of hares, like me," repeated Little Hare. "But a big lion jumped out of the river and gobbled them all up. I am the only one left."

Lion's eyes flashed. "What big lion? I'm the biggest lion there is! Show me this lion!"

"Well ...," said Little Hare. "I don't know ...he's really scary."

Little Hare knocked at Lion's den.

"What?" bellowed Lion.

"My name is Little Hare," said Little Hare. "I am here to be your next meal. More creatures will follow me each day. You will never be hungry again."

"Ho, ho!" roared Lion, flashing his big, shiny teeth. "You will never satisfy my hunger. I will be unsatisfied."

Little Hare's Plan

"You are right to laugh, Lion, sir," said Little Hare unafraid. "The truth is, I lied. I never thought I'd be here all by myself. When I set out, there were many of us."

"There," said Hatch, "if at first you don't succeed, fly, fly again!"

SRA OPEN COURT READING

Ralph, a Bug

by Yve Knick
illustrated by Deborah Colvin Borgo

Bug in a Jar 3
Not a Chicken............................9

Book 28

A Division of The McGraw-Hill Companies
Columbus, Ohio

SRA OPEN COURT READING

www.sra4kids.com

SRA/McGraw-Hill

A Division of The ***McGraw-Hill*** *Companies*

Printed in the United States of America.

Send all inquiries to:
SRA/McGraw-Hill
8787 Orion Place
Columbus, OH 43240-4027

Ralph hopped higher up than before and . . .
WHISH! Ralph flew out the top of the jar.

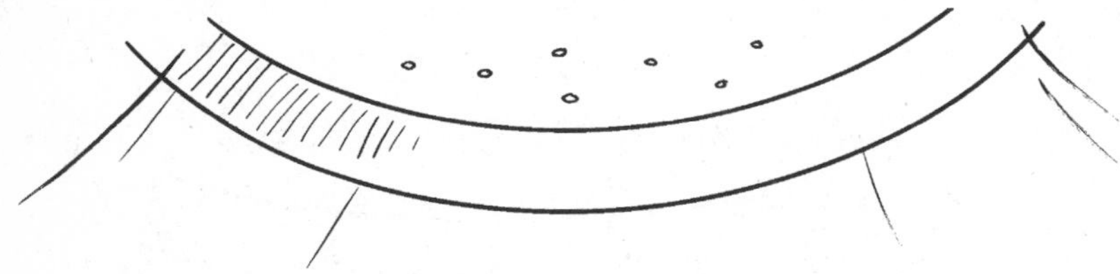

"Cluck, cluck, cluck!" clucked Hatch.

"Stop! I am not a chicken!" yelled Ralph. "I will try again, but just you wait. I'll end up with more cuts and scratches. Stand back!"

Bug in a Jar

Ralph, a bug, sat upon a pinkish-red cattail. It was a blissful day, and a robin sang a song. Ralph was resting in the sun when . . .

Ralph was plucked from his spot. He felt himself being lifted up.

PLOP! Ralph landed in a thick, glass jar.

"Are you chicken?" asked Hatch.

"I am not chicken," said Ralph, "but six is my limit."

"It's such a blissful day," said Hatch. "You can't sit in a glass jar. Try again."

"Not again," grumbled Ralph. "Six is my limit. I'd just hop up and hit the top again. Then I'd hit the bottom. I am scratched and nicked. I am a wreck!"

With a twist of a wrist, a lid was set on top of the jar.

"I am stuck in this jar," said Ralph. "Shucks! I didn't think that he could catch me!"

Ralph sat thinking.

"I will get out. I must get out. I will hop up higher than high and fly."

Ralph hopped up and . . .

BANG! Ralph hit the top. Then Ralph fell lower than low.

THUMP! Ralph hit the bottom.

But Ralph had to get out. Ralph hopped up and . . .

"Try again," said Hatch.

"Not again," grumbled Ralph. "Six is my limit. I'd hop up and hit the highest top with a BANG! Then, THUMP, I'd hit the lowest bottom."

Ralph blinked at his pal who looked a bit odd.
"Can't," Ralph said. "I am stuck in this jar."
"Did you try to hop and fly?" asked Hatch.
"Yup," said Ralph.

CRASH! Ralph hit the top. Then . . .
WHAM! Ralph hit the bottom.
Ralph had a scratched chin and a nicked lip. He had hit his chest and bumped his leg. He was a wreck.

"Six is my limit. I'm finished," said Ralph, and gave up. Ralph wrapped himself up in the grass to nap for a bit.

Not a Chicken

PLINK PLINK! Ralph's pal, Hatch, a wren, pecked at the thick glass.

"Ralph, get up. It's such a blissful day. Let's frolic in the sun!"

The next day Kitty stormed into the house as usual. But this time she closed the door as gently as a breeze.

Kitty smiled. "Mom, I had the best day."

Kitty and the Nothing Day

by Dina & Tim
illustrated by Kersti Frigell

Mom Wants to Know 3
Kitty Tells All.............................8

Book 29

A Division of The McGraw-Hill Companies
Columbus, Ohio

www.sra4kids.com
SRA/McGraw-Hill
A Division of The **McGraw-Hill** *Companies*

Printed in the United States of America.

Send all inquiries to:
SRA/McGraw-Hill
8787 Orion Place
Columbus, OH 43240-4027

"And then in soccer practice, your team lost zero to zero because there was no ball!" Mrs. O'Connor went on with her own version of the story.

"Okay, okay," said Kitty.

"And you read nothing because there were no books! And in music class, when everyone tried to sing, nothing came out! And. . . ."

"Okay! Okay!" Kitty cried. "It was a NOTHING DAY!" Kitty jumped up the steps to her room.

Mrs. O'Connor's eyes opened wide. "Why, that's remarkable!" she gasped. "What did the kids say when they saw it? Did you carry it in your backpack?"

"Mom!" cried Kitty, her hands over her ears. She backed out of the kitchen, laughing. Mrs. O'Connor was laughing, too. What a reaction!

Mom Wants to Know

Every day after school, Kitty O'Connor came in the door and slammed it too hard. She seemed to be looking for an argument. She stamped into the kitchen. She was always starving after school.

Kitty's mom was always there, holding out a glass of milk and a plate of cookies and asking, "So, what did you do in school today?"

Mrs. O'Connor clucked in amazement.

"Now may I go upstairs? I need to call Jane."

"But, Kitty," said Mrs. O'Connor, "what about show-and-tell? Tell me your version."

"Right," Kitty said. "We had show-and-tell. I brought in nothing. Now may I go?"

"So *that's* why you're so hungry!" said Mrs. O'Connor. "And what about the rest of the day?"

"We had a math test. But there were no addition or division problems. I got a zero."

"Nothing" was all Kitty ever said. But that didn't stop Mrs. O'Connor from asking.

Today was no different.

"Nothing?" asked Kitty's mom with amusement.

"That's right," replied Kitty.

"Nothing happened on the way to school?"

"No, Mom. Nothing," Kitty said in agreement.

"Then it was lunchtime. I picked up my tray and looked down at my plate. 'What is this called?' I asked the lunchroom lady."

"What did she say?"

"She said it was the Nothing Special. I didn't eat it."

"At recess," Kitty went on, "no one was in the play yard. So I thought, 'Good, now I can have the best swing all to myself!' "

"That seems like fun!"

"But the equipment was gone! The swings were gone! No slide, no seesaw, no monkey bars—nothing!"

"Dear me!" gasped Mrs. O'Connor in amazement.

"That's terrible," said Mrs. O'Connor. "The trees, dogs, and all the people must have disappeared."

Kitty grinned. "Yes, it was one big, empty space."

Kitty's mom laughed. "Now tell me about school."

Kitty Tells All

"Well, to begin with, there was no school there."

"Nothing at all?" asked Mrs. O'Connor.

"No classrooms, no walls. No education! I just stood there."

"And did nothing," added Mrs. O'Connor.

"Right. That is, until recess."

"Recess. More cookies, Kitty?" asked Mrs. O'Connor. Kitty took two.

Where will you go,
shimmering star,
glittering across the sky?

How far will you go,
traveling star,
flickering across the sky?

SRA Open Court Reading

Traveling Star

by Phillip Ward
illustrated by Mark Corcoran

Shimmering Star 3
Traveling Far 12

Book 30

A Division of The McGraw-Hill Companies
Columbus, Ohio

SRA OPEN COURT READING

www.sra4kids.com

SRA/McGraw-Hill

A Division of The **McGraw-Hill** *Companies*

Printed in the United States of America.

Send all inquiries to:
SRA/McGraw-Hill
8787 Orion Place
Columbus, OH 43240-4027

Imagine! A glittering star. A shimmering star traveling far! All this thinking and imagining! Let a shimmering star surprise you!

Tom started to finish his newly thought of poem.
"How far will you go,
traveling star,
flickering across the sky?"

SRA Open Court Reading

Shimmering Star

Tom gazed at the stars. He was thinking of something to write for class—a truly good poem.

Flashing across the glittering sky was a big, shimmering star! "Where will the shimmering star go?" Tom whispered. "Where will it travel?" He really wanted to know.

Traveling Far

Tom sat up with a start. He had slept much too long! With all this thinking and imagining, at last Tom had all the words for a glittering star poem.

Tom started to write his poem.
"Where will you go,
lovable, shimmering star,
glittering across the sky?"

Tom was thinking much too long. His head started to nod dully.

The glittering star can travel to unimaginable places. Imagine where a traveling star can go! With much thinking and imagining, a shimmering star can travel far!

Tom traveled far with the glittering, shimmering star. He is standing on a wonderfully large wall of blocks.

The glittering star and Tom had unbelievable places to go.

There is no end to where the shimmering star and Tom can go. In glittering Paris, Tom and the traveling star danced madly.

The shimmering star and Tom traveled to London. Big Ben, the clock, rings its bells. Where shall the traveling star and Tom go next? Will they go under the sizable bridge?

Today, fewer than 10,000 blue whales survive. For every blue whale alive today, there used to be twenty. Blue whales continue to be protected. You can see them off the California coast in late summer.

Whales

by Barbara Seiger
illustrated by Meryl Henderson

Types of Whales 3
Biggest Whale 11

Book 31

A Division of The McGraw-Hill Companies
Columbus, Ohio

www.sra4kids.com

SRA/McGraw-Hill

A Division of The **McGraw-Hill** *Companies*

Printed in the United States of America.

Send all inquiries to:
SRA/McGraw-Hill
8787 Orion Place
Columbus, OH 43240-4027

At one time blue whales thrived. Whalers hunted blue whales for their meat and useful whale oil. Hunting reached its peak in 1931 and caused a bad situation. By 1966 there were so few blue whales left that a ban was placed on hunting them.

Experts think that blue whales communicate with hums. Adult whales hum in deep, cold water. The cold helps the hums travel better. These hums can travel as far as 100 miles. When humans hear these hums, it seems like an imitation of a joyful song.

Types of Whales

Whales may spend most of their time underwater, but they are quite different from fish. Whales have lungs and smooth skin. Fish breathe with gills and are covered with scales. Whales swim differently, too. Both fish and whales use their tails to swim. But a fish tail goes from side to side while a whale tail goes up and down.

Like humans, whales are mammals. Baby whales don't hatch out of eggs like fish. Baby whales grow inside the mother and are alive during birth. After its birth, the baby stays close to its mother so it can reach her plentiful milk quickly.

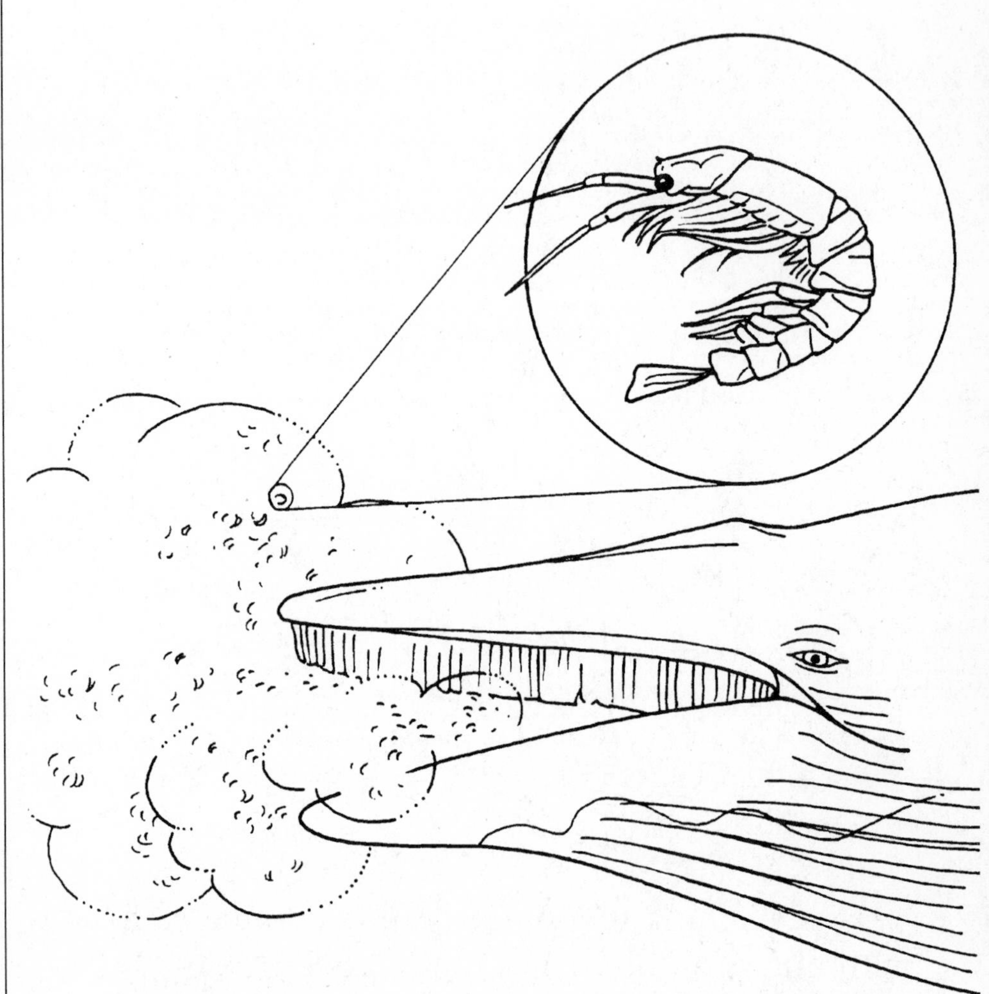

Blue whales must eat a lot. They eat mainly krill, a shrimplike creature. Each whale must consume one to two tons of krill each day.

As huge as it is, the blue whale can still jump up out of the water, and swim on its back. It's quick, too, swimming up to twenty miles per hour. Its strong tail helps the blue whale swim fast and jump high.

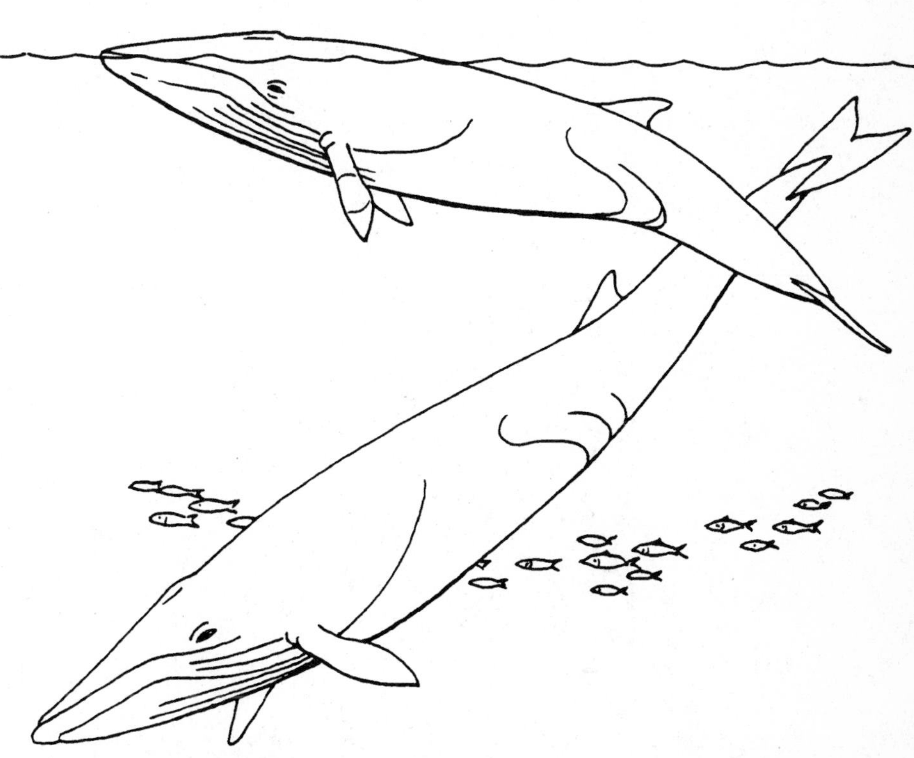

Like other mammals, whales need air. A whale can't breathe in liquid, so it must swim to the top of the water to get air. Before it goes back under, a whale will fill up its lungs just like we do before we dive. Some whales need fresh air frequently. They swim up every two to three minutes. Others, like the piked whale, can stay underwater for longer—120 minutes.

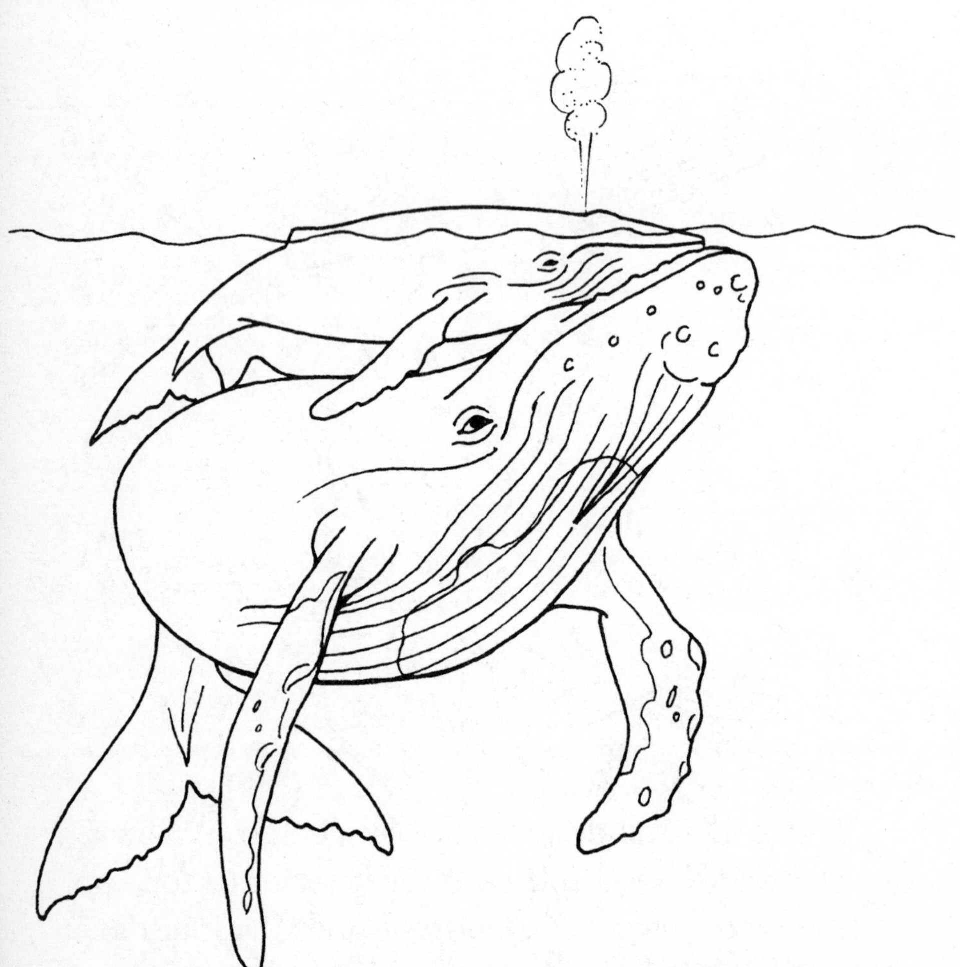

During birth, a baby whale doesn't breathe. As soon as it is born, the baby must swim up and fill its lungs with air. If a new baby has difficulty swimming, the mother will carefully help.

Biggest Whale

Blue whales are huge. In fact, they are bigger than any other creature. A blue whale can be more than 100 feet long, but most are 70–90 feet. This is longer than four buses placed end to end. Blue whales can weigh up to 150 tons. Lifting a blue whale would be like picking up more than thirty elephants.

Baleen whales have no teeth. In place of teeth, they have baleen plates. When the whale feeds, it takes in a lot of water. Then, when it pushes the water back out, the baleen acts as a strainer. Tiny fish that were in the water are left behind for the whale to eat.

When a whale is underwater, air in its lungs gets hot and damp. When a whale needs fresh air, it rises up and blows the old air out of a blowhole on top of its body. When the hot air hits colder outside air, it turns into fog.

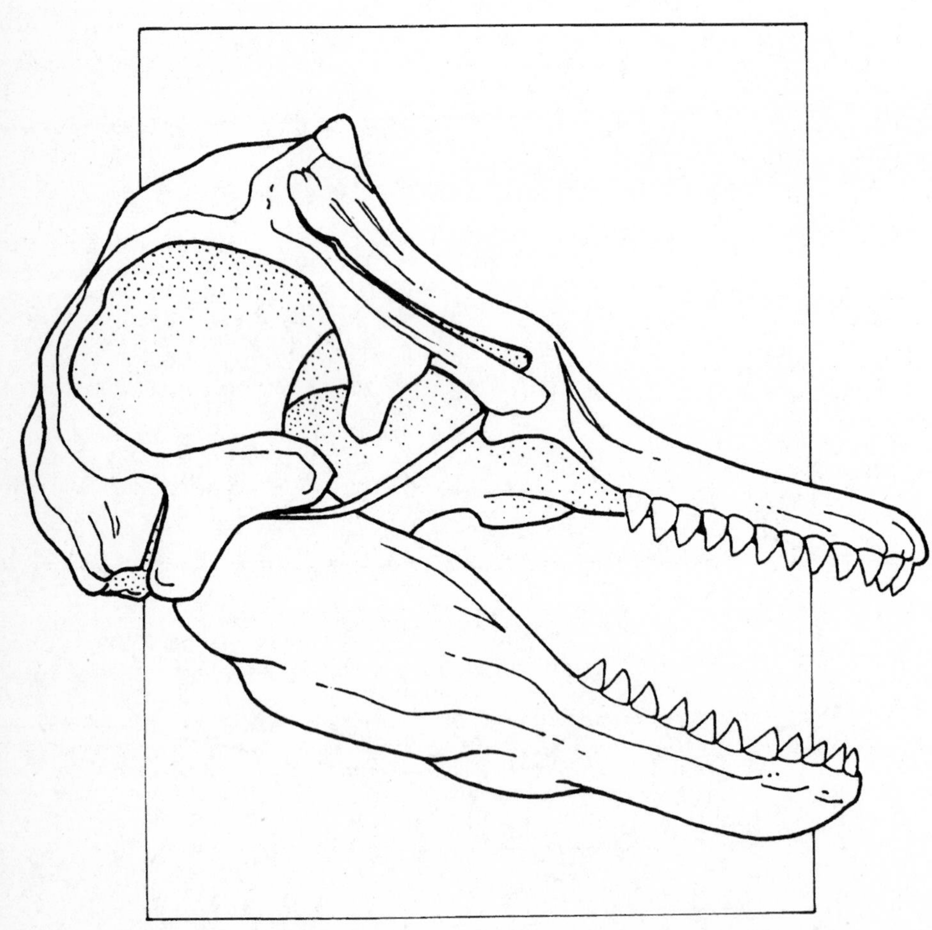

There are two different types of whales, based on how they eat. Some whales have teeth. But they don't use these teeth to chew. These whales use their teeth only to catch their meals.

The killer whale, or orca, is one type of whale with teeth. Orcas have very sharp teeth. The name *killer whale* makes orcas seem scary. But don't be fearful. An orca will not go after humans. It uses its sharp teeth only on whales and fish.

Every animal stopped working and ran to look. They all felt relieved that it was only a herd of horses galloping by. They looked at each other and smiled happily.

The Stone Wall

by Aleta Naylor
illustrated by Jan Pyk

The Rumbling 3
The Search 10

Book 32

A Division of The McGraw-Hill Companies
Columbus, Ohio

SRA Open Court Reading

www.sra4kids.com

SRA/McGraw-Hill

A Division of The McGraw-Hill Companies

Printed in the United States of America.

Send all inquiries to:
SRA/McGraw-Hill
8787 Orion Place
Columbus, OH 43240-4027

The animals took their time, each one looking carefully for just the right spot on the new wall. Getting everything set perfectly took a while. It was quite late when they went to sleep. The next morning they felt tired but very happy. They had just returned to their daily activities when a scary rumbling began.

Just when they had lost all hope of finding a new home, they came to a brook bordered by an old stone wall. All misgivings suddenly left them, and they felt quite pleased. Raccoon thought that this new stone wall was perfect. It was just like the old home.

The Rumbling

Chief Raccoon thought Stone Wall was perfect. Everyone got along wonderfully with each other, and that's what he liked most. Every morning birds sang in the trees, and the farmer led his horses out to graze. Raccoon's community enjoyed complete peace.

Then one awful morning the horses didn't appear. The animals felt fearful for one brief moment but decided that the farmer might just be leading his horses to a different field that day. They went on with their daily activities like always.

The animals roamed the field for quite a while but did not decide on anything. There was plenty of bright sunlight, but no lilies and no ivies. It was getting late, and it would be dark soon. The animals were all in bad moods.

Someone suggested that they make their new home in the beautiful woods. So they tried different places all day long, but no place seemed quite right. It was just too gloomy. Their old home at Stone Wall got lots of sunlight. Raccoon suggested that they try the field. The field always got plenty of light.

The next day, loud rumbling filled the air. The animals didn't know what to make of it. But when night came, all rumbling stopped. The animals went to sleep, believing that everything might still be okay in the morning.

When morning came, the animals woke to more rumbling. Now they were fearful. They all came to see Chief Raccoon. Raccoon told them he would find what was making the noise.

Chief Raccoon told them not to be fearful. They would look for a new home. He believed they would find relief.

The Search

There was no time left, and the animals had to go. They ran as fast as they could. At the edge of the woods, they stopped to take one last tearful look at their home. Stone Wall was demolished, and they knew that they could never return.

Chief Raccoon and Skunk went to the field. At the top of the hill, they saw the cause of all that rumbling. Three huge monsters, unlike anything they had ever seen, were eating up everything in their paths. Not a piece was left.

When Chief Raccoon and Skunk got home, all the animals were waiting for them. He did not deceive them. Some animals were fearful and voted to leave right away. Others felt that it might be a mistake to leave their perfect home at Stone Wall.

They debated until the sun began to light the sky. When the rumbling started again, the animals were still undecided. But then the monsters appeared on the hilltop. They were aimed at the stone wall! The animals could not believe it.

Flags are also used in car races. Car races are noisy, and the drivers can't hear. They need a code they can see. If there is trouble on the track, an official waves a yellow flag. This tells the drivers to slow down. A checkered flag is waved when the winning race car crosses the finish line.

Old codes continue to be used, as new codes are invented. Someday, you may create a code of your own to enjoy and share.

Say It in Code

by Kacie Jones
illustrated by Meryl Henderson

Communicating in Code 3
Say It with Flags 10

Book 33

A Division of The McGraw-Hill Companies
Columbus, Ohio

SRA OPEN COURT READING

www.sra4kids.com

SRA/McGraw-Hill

A Division of The **McGraw-Hill** *Companies*

Printed in the United States of America.

Send all inquiries to:
SRA/McGraw-Hill
8787 Orion Place
Columbus, OH 43240-4027

Small Craft Warning
winds up to
38 miles per hour

Gale Warning
winds from
39 to 54 miles per hour

Storm Warning
winds from
55 to 73 miles per hour

Hurricane Warning
winds at least
74 miles per hour

Flags are used to signal boaters when bad weather looms. Storm warning flags warn boaters of strong winds. When boaters see the warning flags, they can head for safety.

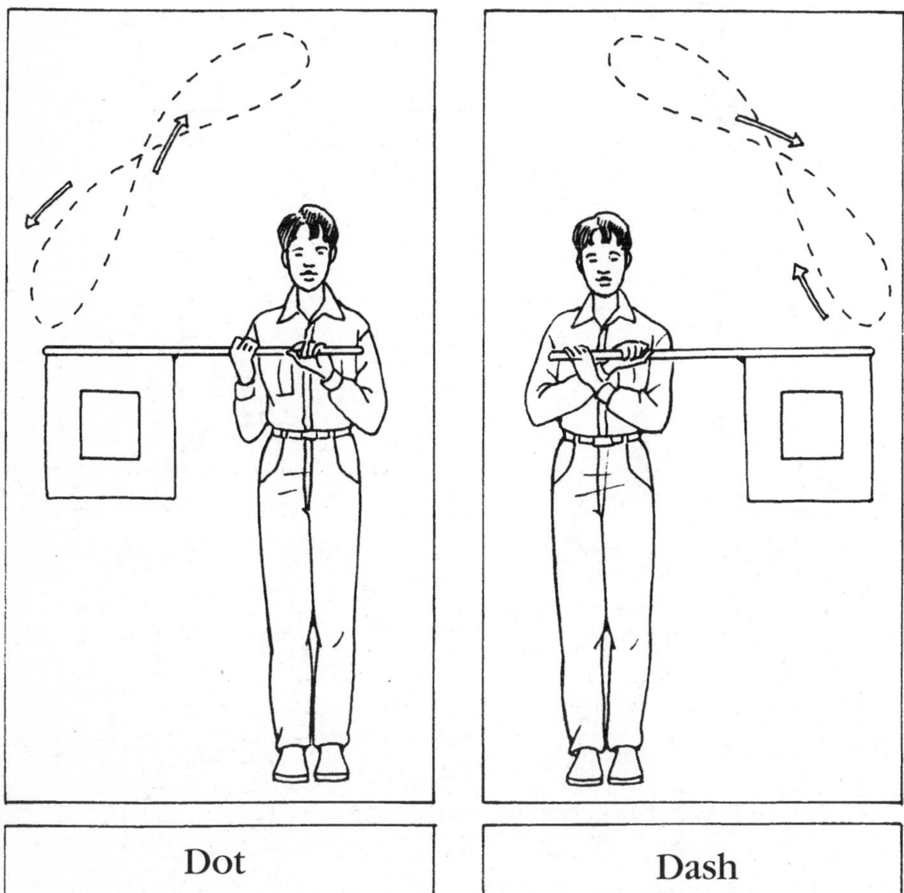

A flag can also be used to send Morse code. The flag is moved one way to mean a dot and moved another way to mean a dash. This code, called *wigwag,* is slow and is not used very much.

Communicating in Code

Have you ever written yourself a note or drawn pictures that nobody else could understand? Or spoken so that only one person understood? If so, you were using a code.

A code is like a language. Codes can be very simple—or very complicated. Codes can work by switching letters of the alphabet.

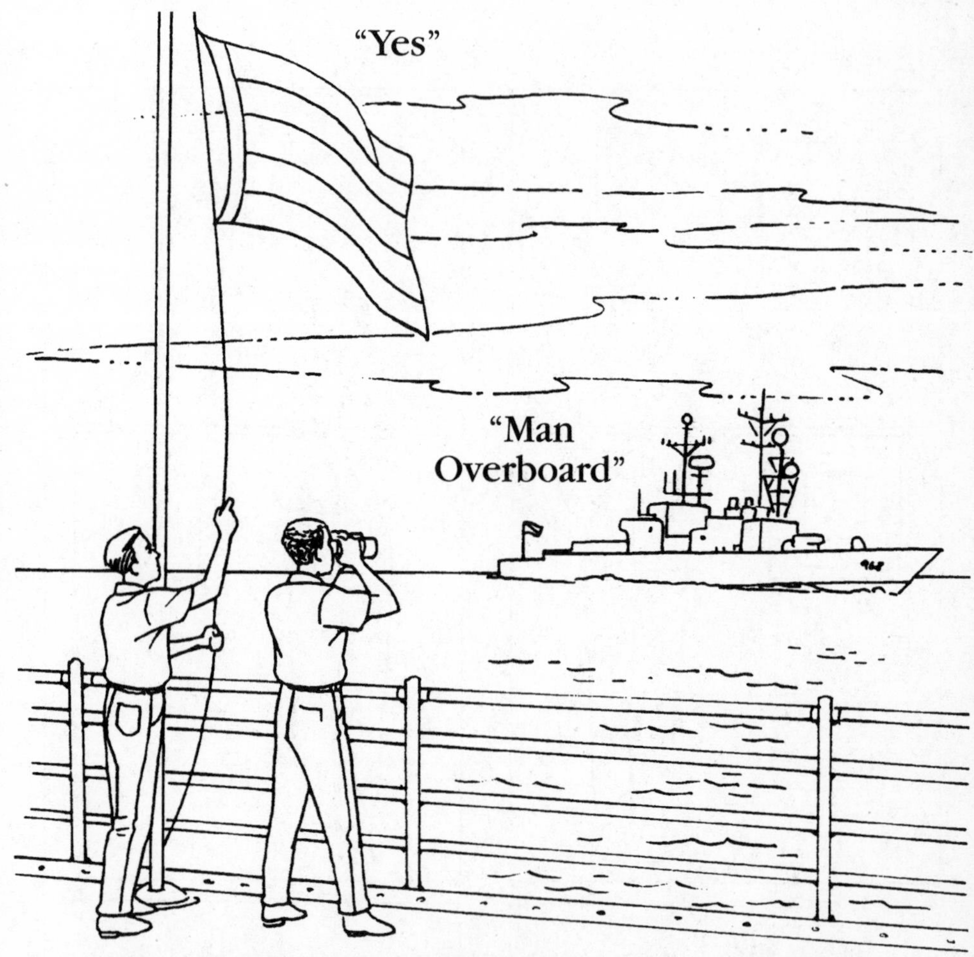

Each international flag also stands for a phrase. For example, the flag for the letter O also means "man overboard." The flag for the letter C also means "yes." People have to be able to read the messages correctly.

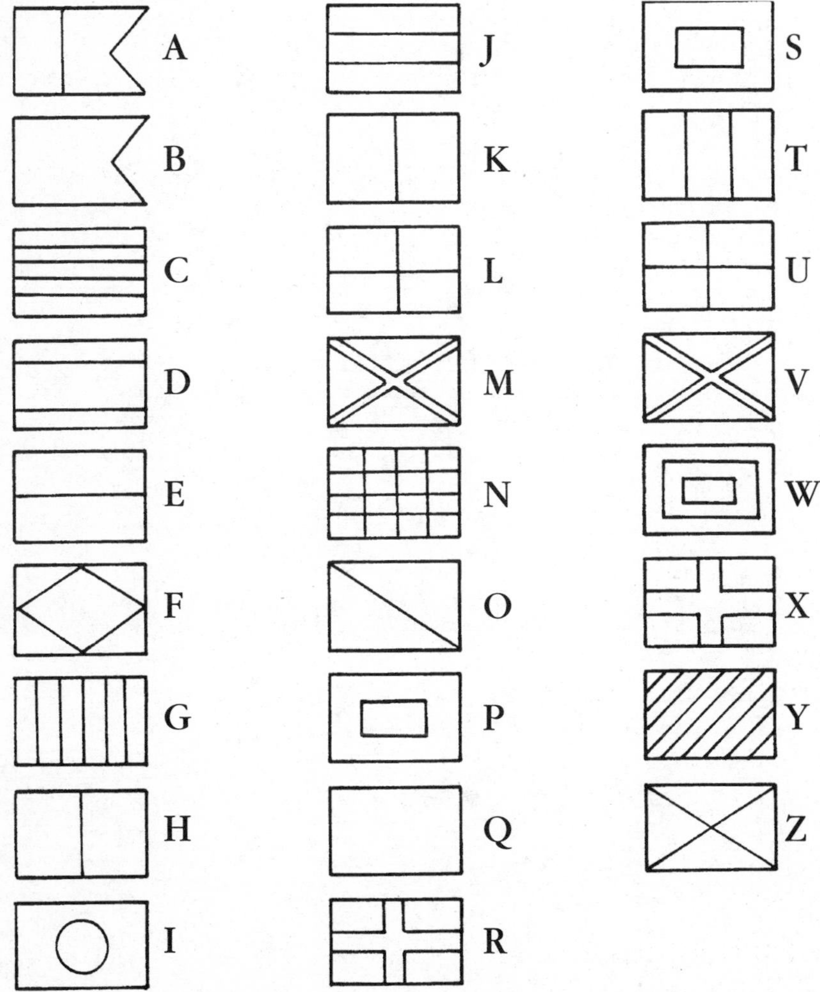

The international flag code is used around the world. Each flag stands for a letter of the alphabet. Sailors join two to five flags together with clips to spell a word or a code meaning.

Codes can use patterns of beeps
or dots
or hand signals
or flags
or even flashlights.

Codes have been used since before colonial times. Before telephones were invented, the telegraph was used. Messages were sent on the telegraph using Morse code. Each letter of the alphabet in Morse code is made up of dots and dashes.

The positions of the flags stand for letters and numbers. Red-and-yellow flags are used at sea. Red-and-white flags are used on land.

Say It with Flags

Flags have been used for thousands of years to send codes. Sailors use two flags to send semaphore code.

Some codes are easy to figure out. Other codes take teams of trained experts a long time to "crack." For thousands of years, armies have used codes to prevent enemies from knowing secret battle plans.

Another type of code was invented to help people who can't see read books. It is called Braille and is a special system of printing. Raised dots form the letters of the alphabet. People who can't see read by touching the dots with their fingers.

People who do not hear well use a code called sign language. Communicating is done using hands. Words and letters are made with hand shapes and movements.

Finally, Becky could think. Finally, she had peace and quiet.

Peace and Quiet

by Chloe Texier-Rose
illustrated by Len Epstein

Becky's Problem........................3
Mom's Plan................................8

Book 34

A Division of The McGraw-Hill Companies

Columbus, Ohio

www.sra4kids.com

SRA/McGraw-Hill

A Division of The ***McGraw-Hill*** *Companies*

Printed in the United States of America.

Send all inquiries to:
SRA/McGraw-Hill
8787 Orion Place
Columbus, OH 43240-4027

So, Becky did what her mom said. Suddenly her room seemed so quiet. Her sisters were still playing on their beds, but they didn't seem as loud. Her brothers were still arguing next door, but they seemed miles away. The TV still blared, but Becky could barely hear it. Even the train passing outside her window seemed far away. And you know what?

"Mom!" Becky wailed. "How can this help? I have even less peace and quiet!"

Mom smiled. "I have one last thing for you to do. Ask Daddy to take out the radio, TV, computer, and stereo. Give your brothers their pets back. Ask Grandma and Grandpa to sleep in their own room. Then let's see what happens."

Mom's ideas had not worked so far, but Becky was resigned to try this one last thing. "Okay, Mom," she muttered.

Becky's Problem

In Becky's apartment the dog was barking, the baby was crying, her dad was shouting, her grandma was snoring, the television was blaring, and her mom was cooking, clanking pots and pans.

Becky went into her room. She shared it with two sisters. Her sisters were there, playing, laughing, and singing. She could hear her brothers' argument in the next room. Becky had homework to do. But how could she think with all this noise? She needed peace and quiet.

Becky complained to her mom. Mom just smiled and reminded Becky of her promise. Then, she told Becky to put all the family pets in her room. She also had Becky get more pink pillows so Grandma and Grandpa could sleep in her room, too.

Becky did as she was told. But nothing got better. With the television, radio, stereo, and computer in her room, there was barely space for Becky. All ten people in her family were in her room almost all the time. Confusion reigned.

Becky went into the kitchen. "Mom," she said. "Things couldn't be worse. I can't think. I need peace and quiet. I can't write like this. I can't do my schoolwork."

Mom looked at Becky. "What can we do, Becky? We have a lot of people living in our apartment. There are ten people, Becky. I can't assign a room to you."

"But, Mom," Becky groaned. "I need my own space. I need peace and quiet. I need my own room."

"I know, baby," Becky's mom agreed. "I need the same treatment. But it's just not possible right now."

"But, Mom," Becky cried. "I need things to be better."

Becky went back to Mom. "Mom," she started, "I don't understand. How did this help? Now everything is worse."

Mom smiled at her daughter. "Becky, you promised to do what I say, no matter what. Remember? Now go get the radio. Ask Daddy to get the stereo and the computer. Take them all into your room."

"But, Mom . . ."

"Don't doubt me. Just do it, Becky."

"But I doubt that will solve the problem," Becky said to herself. It was great having the TV. But now everyone came into her room to watch. Becky had even less peace and quiet.

"Okay," Mom said. "I have an idea. But you have to trust me. You have to do whatever I say, no matter what your doubts."

Becky didn't know what her mom had planned, but she trusted her. Besides, things couldn't get worse. "Okay," Becky said. "What do I do?"

Mom's Plan

Just as Becky's mom opened her mouth to tell Becky the plan, Grandma let out a huge snore that shook the glass in all the windows. Outside, the train roared by on its elevated tracks. The whole apartment shook down to the pavement.

"The first thing you do is ask Daddy to take the TV out of the living room and put it in your bedroom."

"Thank you!" Becky was overjoyed. The TV in her room! She'd always wanted that. "Okay, Mom," she exclaimed. "Okay!"

After school, children went home and did their evening chores. Then the family ate supper and spent the evening together. Bedtime was welcome after such a long day. The children would need a good night's rest to rise at dawn to begin a new day.

School Days Long Ago

by Jean Phillips
illustrated by Gary Undercuffler

One-Room Schoolhouse.............3
School Days, School Days.........10

Book 35

A Division of The McGraw-Hill Companies
Columbus, Ohio

SRA OPEN COURT READING

www.sra4kids.com

SRA/McGraw-Hill

A Division of The **McGraw-Hill** *Companies*

Printed in the United States of America.

Send all inquiries to:
SRA/McGraw-Hill
8787 Orion Place
Columbus, OH 43240-4027

Girls liked to play hopscotch, sing songs, and play with cornhusk dolls. The boys played marbles, tag, or football. Football was a rough game and was played with a stuffed leather sack. The children also liked to play hide-and-seek.

Children carried their lunches in tin pails or baskets, or tied in cloth. Homemade bread and jam were packed. Drinking water came from the well.

At recess, games were often made up and needed little equipment. Leftover wood and string were used to make spinning tops. Hoops from barrels were used in races and other games.

One-Room Schoolhouse

Can you imagine going to school in 1776? That was a long, long time ago—more than 200 years ago, in fact. Getting an education was very different back then.

Schools in those days were very small. Most had only a single room. One teacher taught all the children. Students were in grades one through eight and were from six to twenty years old. Enrollment was usually small.

Later in the afternoon, older students worked on spelling, reading, and arithmetic while younger ones practiced the alphabet. Because paper and books were scarce, students learned to do addition, subtraction, division, and multiplication in their heads.

Good penmanship, or neat handwriting, was an important skill for a farmer, storekeeper, or craftsperson. Children used a slate pencil to copy their writing lesson from the blackboard onto a small slate. Later, they used a quill pen and an inkpot to copy it into their copybooks in their best handwriting.

The teacher arrived early to sweep and clean the entire classroom. In winter, the building was kept warm with a fireplace or a wood-burning stove. Parents provided the firewood. Each morning, a different student would start the fire before the other children arrived.

Before coming to school, many children had chores to do at home. The environment was harsh. The children walked miles to school or rode horses. There were no school buses, cars, or pavement.

One book, called a primer, contained the alphabet, numbers, spelling words, and poems. During the first part of the day, the teacher worked with the younger ones. Older students worked on their own, studying and writing in their copybooks by themselves. Copybook paper had no lines. Students had to draw their own straight lines on the paper before they could write.

School Days, School Days

Schoolbooks were in short supply, so children shared. In some schools there might be only one book for the whole class. Students often memorized their lessons, then recited them to the class.

The teacher would ring a bell to signal the beginning of the school day. If there were two doors, girls would enter the school through one door, and boys would come in the other. Students had to stand outside until after recess if they were late.

School started at eight o'clock each morning and ended nine hours later at five o'clock. If there were many students, the younger children would go to the summer session. The older students would go to the winter session.

During the school day children were expected to be as quiet as mice. With many ages in the classroom, it was important that students behaved. If a student disturbed the class or was rude to the teacher, the teacher would keep the student in for recess. The student might also have to stay after school.